Mastering Managerial Skills for Success

Dr. Preeti Gupta

Contents

Acknowledgment

Introduction

Module 1: Introduction to Managerial Skills   1

> ➢ Overview of Managerial Skills: Technical, Human Relations, and Conceptual.
> ➢ Role of Managerial Skills in Achieving Organizational Goals.
> ➢ Importance of Balancing these Skills for Effective Management.

Module 2: Human Relations Skills   8

> ➢ Importance of Human Relations Skills (soft skills) in Managerial Roles.
> ➢ Key Components: Communication, Empathy, Conflict Resolution, Teamwork, Motivation.
> ➢ Practical Tips for Enhancing Human Relations Skills through Practice and Feedback.

Module 3: Conceptual Skills   19

> ➢ Conceptual Skills in Strategic Management and Decision- Making.
> ➢ How Conceptual Skills Differ at Different Managerial Levels (from front-line to executive).
> ➢ Techniques for Improving Strategic Thinking and Long-Term Planning Abilities.

Module 4: Technical Skills   30

> ➢ Definition and Examples of Technical Skills Relevant to Different Functional Areas.

➤ Importance of Technical skills at Various Managerial Levels. How to Develop and Maintain Technical Expertise in a Rapidly Changing Environment.

Module 5: Global Management Skills   43

➤ Understanding the Importance of Global Management Skills in Today's Interconnected World.

➤ Challenges and Opportunities in Global Business Environments.

➤ Strategies for Developing Cross-Cultural Competence and Managing International Teams.

Module 6: Leadership and Influence   52

➤ Characteristics of Effective Leadership in Managerial Roles.

➤ Different Leadership Styles and Their Impact on Team Performance.

➤ Techniques for Inspiring and Motivating Teams to Achieve Goals.

Module 7: Problem Solving and Decision-Making Skills   65

➤ Frameworks for Systematic Problem-Solving and Decision-Making

➤ How to Gather Relevant Information, Analyze Options, and Implement Solutions

➤ Case Studies or Examples Illustrating Effective Problem-Solving Techniques.

Module 8: Time and Stress Management   72

➤ Strategies to manage time and Stress

➤ Techniques for Reducing Stress and Maintaining Work-Life Balance

➤ Tools and Resources for Enhancing Personal Productivity and Resilience

Module 9: Communication and Presentation Skills   83

  ➤ Importance of Clear and Effective Communication in Managerial Roles

  ➤ Tips For Improving Written and Verbal Communication Skills

  ➤ Guidelines For Delivering Impactful Presentations to Different Audiences

Module 10: Ethics and Professionalism   92

  ➤ Ethical Considerations in Managerial Decision-Making and Behaviour.

  ➤ Importance Of Maintaining Integrity and Professionalism

  ➤ Case Studies or Scenarios to Facilitate Ethical Reasoning and Decision-Making.

Module 11: Continuous Learning and Development   98

  ➤ The Mindset of Lifelong Learning and Professional Growth.

  ➤ Strategies For Staying Updated on Industry Trends and Best Practices

  ➤ Resources for Ongoing Development, Such as Courses, Books, and Networking.

Module 12: Conclusion and Action Plan   106

  ➤ Summary of Key Takeaways from the Handbook

  ➤ Self-Assessment Tools or Reflection Questions to Gauge Personal Growth and Development.

  ➤ Actionable Steps for Applying Managerial Skills in Daily Practices

Acknowledgments

This book represents a significant milestone in our academic journey, and I are deeply grateful for the steadfast support I have received. My heartfelt appreciation goes to Prof Premanand Shetty, the Chancellor of Alliance University; Mr. Abhay Chebbi, Pro Chancellor; and the leadership team for their continuous support and guidance.

Additionally, I extend heartfelt appreciation to all members of our group, whose collaboration and dedication have been integral to the completion of this work. Everyone's contribution has been invaluable, and I are truly appreciative of the collective effort in this academic pursuit.

In conclusion, I wish to express our sincere gratitude to all individuals who, as part of a collective effort, have played a direct or indirect role in the completion of this significant work. Your contributions have been invaluable, and I am deeply appreciative of your involvement in this academic endeavour.

Introduction

Mastering Essential Managerial Skills for Success is a comprehensive guide designed to equip managers with the crucial skills needed to excel in their roles. It takes readers on an immersive journey through modern management. The handbook emphasizes the importance of balancing technical, human relations, and conceptual skills to achieve organizational goals effectively.

It covers essential human relations skills such as communication, empathy, conflict resolution, teamwork, and motivation, providing practical tips for enhancement. The guide also explores conceptual skills necessary for strategic management and decision-making, discussing their significance at various managerial levels.

Technical skills relevant to different functional areas like marketing, finance, and operations are discussed, along with strategies for developing expertise in a rapidly changing environment. The handbook addresses global management skills, highlighting the importance of cross-cultural competence and strategies for managing international teams.

Leadership and influence are examined, detailing effective leadership characteristics, styles, and techniques for team motivation. It also delves into problem-solving and decision-making, offering systematic approaches and illustrative case studies.

Time and stress management strategies are provided, along with tips for improving communication and presentation skills. The importance of ethics and professionalism in managerial roles is emphasized through ethical considerations and case studies. The handbook encourages continuous learning and development, offering strategies for staying updated and resources for ongoing growth. It concludes with key takeaways, actionable steps, and self-assessment tools for personal development.

Module 1

Introduction to Managerial Skills

Definition

Managerial skills incorporate the knowledge and abilities essential for individuals in managerial roles to effectively perform various management tasks. These skills are crucial for achieving success in the key functions of management: planning, organizing, leading, and controlling. They can broadly be categorized into technical skills, human relations skills, and conceptual skills, each playing a distinct role depending on the manager's level within an organization. Furthermore, in today's interconnected and globalized business landscape, managers face unique challenges that necessitate the development of specialized global management skills.

Technical Skills:

Technical skills refer to the proficiency and expertise in a specific field or discipline. For managers, these skills are particularly relevant at lower levels of the organizational hierarchy, where they are often directly involved in performing tasks and overseeing operations related to their area of expertise. In practical terms, technical skills enable managers to understand and effectively utilize the tools, techniques, and procedures required to accomplish specific tasks within their functional domain.

For example, a marketing manager needs strong technical skills in market analysis, advertising strategies, and digital marketing platforms to effectively plan and execute marketing campaigns. Similarly, an engineering manager relies on technical skills in project management, product design, and technology implementation to ensure the successful development and delivery of engineering projects.

Human Relations Skills:

Human relations skills, also known as interpersonal or soft skills, are essential for managers at all levels of an organization. These skills involve the ability to communicate effectively, motivate employees, build relationships, and resolve conflicts in a constructive manner.

Human relations skills are crucial in fostering a positive work environment, enhancing teamwork, and promoting employee morale and productivity.

Managers with strong human relations skills can inspire trust and cooperation among team members, thereby improving overall organizational performance. These skills are particularly critical in leadership roles where the manager's ability to understand and respond to the needs and concerns of employees directly impacts team dynamics and organizational culture.

Conceptual Skills:

Conceptual skills involve the ability to think strategically, analyze complex situations, and make sound decisions based on a comprehensive understanding of the organization as a whole. These skills are most relevant at higher levels of management, where managers are responsible for setting goals, formulating long-term strategies, and adapting to changes in the external business environment.

Conceptual skills enable managers to envision the future direction of the organization, identify opportunities for growth and innovation, and anticipate potential challenges. Managers with strong conceptual skills are adept at synthesizing information, evaluating alternatives, and developing cohesive plans that align with the organization's mission and objectives.

Global Management Skills:

In today's globalized business environment, managers must possess specialized skills to effectively navigate the complexities of international markets, cultural diversity, and geopolitical factors. Global management skills go beyond technical, human relations, and conceptual skills by encompassing a deeper understanding of global trends, cross-cultural communication, international regulations, and strategic alliances.

Managers with global management skills are capable of leading multicultural teams, adapting management practices to diverse cultural norms, and identifying opportunities for international expansion or collaboration. These skills are essential for addressing global challenges such as market volatility, political instability, and differences in business practices across countries.

Integration of Managerial Skills:

Successful managers recognize the interconnectedness of these skills and their importance in achieving organizational goals. For instance, while technical skills provide the foundation for performing specific tasks, human relations skills facilitate effective communication and collaboration among team members, thereby enhancing productivity and morale. Conceptual skills enable managers to formulate strategic plans that leverage their technical expertise and align with the organization's long-term objectives.

Moreover, the emphasis on each type of skill may vary depending on the manager's level within the organizational hierarchy. Entry-level managers typically rely more on technical skills to execute operational tasks, whereas senior executives draw heavily on conceptual skills to shape the organization's strategic direction. Human relations skills, however, remain relevant across all managerial levels as they are fundamental to building strong interpersonal relationships and fostering a cohesive organizational culture.

Conclusion:

In conclusion, managerial skills encompass a diverse set of competencies that are essential for effectively planning, organizing, leading, and controlling within an organization. These skills—technical, human relations, conceptual, and global management—play complementary roles in enabling managers to navigate challenges, drive innovation, and achieve sustainable growth in an increasingly complex business environment. By developing and honing these skills, managers can enhance their effectiveness, inspire high performance among employees, and contribute to the long-term success of their organizations.

1. **Role of Managerial Skills in Achieving Organizational Goals**

- The role of managerial skills in achieving organizational goals cannot be overstated. Effective management is the backbone of any successful organization, and it relies heavily on the combination of technical, human relations, and conceptual skills.
- **Strategic Planning and Execution**: Conceptual skills are crucial for strategic planning and execution. Managers need to have a deep understanding of the organization's mission, vision, and goals. They must be able to analyze the internal and external environments, identify opportunities and threats, and develop strategies to achieve the organization's objectives. Once the strategy is in place, managers use their technical and human relations skills to implement the plan. For example, a marketing manager might use their technical skills to develop a marketing campaign and their human relations skills to lead a team to execute the campaign effectively.
- **Effective Communication and Team Building**: Human relations skills play a vital role in building strong teams and fostering effective communication. Managers need to communicate the organization's goals and objectives clearly to their teams, ensuring that everyone understands their role in achieving these goals. They must also be able to motivate and inspire their teams, creating a positive work environment where employees feel valued and engaged. Strong human relations skills help managers resolve conflicts, build trust, and promote collaboration, which are essential for achieving organizational goals.
- **Operational Efficiency**: Technical skills are essential for maintaining operational efficiency. Managers need to understand the technical aspects of their work to ensure that processes are running smoothly and efficiently. They must be able to identify and solve technical problems, optimize processes, and implement best practices. For example, an operations manager in a manufacturing plant needs to have technical knowledge of the production process to ensure that the plant operates efficiently and meets production targets.
- **Innovation and Problem Solving**: Conceptual skills are also important for innovation and problem-solving. Managers need

to be able to think creatively and come up with innovative solutions to challenges. They must be able to analyze complex problems, consider various options, and make decisions that align with the organization's goals. For example, a product development manager might use their conceptual skills to develop a new product that meets customer needs and supports the organization's growth objectives.

3. Importance of Balancing These Skills for Effective Management

Balancing technical, human relations, and conceptual skills is crucial for effective management. While each of these skills is important on its own, it is the combination and balance of these skills that enable managers to perform their roles effectively.

- **Adaptability and Flexibility**: Managers need to be adaptable and flexible, able to switch between different skills depending on the situation. For example, a manager might need to use their technical skills to solve a specific problem, their human relations skills to motivate their team, and their conceptual skills to develop a strategic plan. The ability to balance these skills allows managers to respond effectively to different challenges and opportunities.
- **Leadership and Decision Making**: Effective leadership and decision-making require a balance of all three skills. Managers need to use their technical skills to understand the details of their work, their human relations skills to lead and motivate their teams, and their conceptual skills to make strategic decisions. For example, a CEO needs to have a broad understanding of the organization's operations, the ability to communicate and inspire employees, and the ability to make strategic decisions that drive the organization's success.
- **Building a Positive Organizational Culture**: Balancing these skills is also important for building a positive organizational culture. Managers who can effectively combine technical expertise, strong interpersonal skills, and strategic thinking can create an environment where employees feel supported and valued. This, in turn, leads to higher employee engagement, satisfaction, and productivity.

- **Achieving Long-term Success**: The long-term success of an organization depends on its ability to adapt to changing circumstances and continuously improve. Managers who can balance technical, human relations, and conceptual skills are better equipped to drive continuous improvement, foster innovation, and ensure that the organization remains competitive. For example, a manager who can effectively balance these skills might be able to lead a successful change initiative, implement new technologies, or develop new products that drive the organization's growth.
- In conclusion, technical, human relations, and conceptual skills are all essential for effective management. The ability to balance these skills allows managers to perform their roles effectively, achieve organizational goals, and drive long-term success. By developing and honing these skills, managers can become more effective leaders, build strong teams, and create a positive and productive work environment.

Question bank:

2 Marks Questions:

1. What is meant by Managerial Skills?

2. Define the types of Managerial Skills.

3. What is meant by Human Relation Skills?

4. Give an example of Technical Skill required for a manger.

5. What is meant by Innovative and Problem-Solving Skill?

5 Marks Questions:

1. Discuss the importance of effective Managerial Skills in organizational success.

2. Explain the difference between Conceptual and Technical Skills required for managers role with examples.

3. Describe the importance of balancing these skills for effective management.

4. Can managerial skills really be effective in achieving organisation success? Provide examples from industry.

5. Discuss the importance of managerial skills in achieving long term success.

10 Marks Questions:

1. Discuss the various managerial skill types and how does it apply to business organisation? Provide a real-life example to illustrate each type of the skill sets.

2. Role of managerial skills in achieving organizational goals is impactful and essential. Elaborate.

Module 2

Human Relations Skills

Definition of Human Relations Skills:

Human relations skills, often referred to as soft skills, encompass the abilities required to interact effectively with others, manage relationships, and navigate social complexities in the workplace. These skills include communication, empathy, conflict resolution, teamwork, and motivation. Unlike technical skills, which involve specific knowledge and abilities related to a particular field, human relations skills are more about how managers interact with their teams, colleagues, and stakeholders. These skills are essential for creating a positive work environment, fostering collaboration, and achieving organizational goals.

Importance of Human Relations Skills in Managerial Roles:

- **Enhancing Communication**: Effective communication is the cornerstone of successful management. Managers need to convey information clearly and listen actively to understand the needs and concerns of their team members. Good communication helps prevent misunderstandings, promotes transparency, and builds trust within the team. Managers who excel in communication can articulate the organization's vision and goals, provide constructive feedback, and facilitate open dialogue.
- **Building Trust and Relationships**: Trust is fundamental to any successful team. Managers with strong human relations skills can build and maintain trust by being consistent, reliable, and fair. They understand the importance of building relationships based on mutual respect and understanding. Trustworthy managers create an environment where employees feel safe to express their ideas, take risks, and collaborate freely.
- **Resolving Conflicts**: Conflict is inevitable in any workplace, but how it is managed can significantly impact team dynamics and productivity. Managers with effective conflict resolution skills

8

can address issues promptly and fairly, preventing them from escalating and affecting the team's morale and performance. They use negotiation and mediation techniques to find mutually acceptable solutions and maintain harmony within the team.

- **Enhancing Teamwork and Collaboration**: Teams that work well together are more productive and innovative. Managers play a crucial role in fostering teamwork by encouraging collaboration, facilitating effective communication, and recognizing and leveraging the strengths of each team member. They create an inclusive environment where everyone feels valued and motivated to contribute to the team's success.
- **Motivating and Engaging Employees**: Motivation is a key driver of employee performance and satisfaction. Managers with strong human relations skills understand what motivates their team members and can tailor their management style to meet individual needs. They use positive reinforcement, provide opportunities for growth and development, and create a supportive work environment that encourages employees to perform at their best.
- **Promoting a Positive Organizational Culture**: Organizational culture is shaped by the behaviors, attitudes, and values of its members. Managers with strong human relations skills can influence and promote a positive culture by leading by example, fostering open communication, and encouraging collaboration and innovation. A positive culture enhances employee engagement, satisfaction, and retention.

2. Key Components of Human Relations Skills

- **Communication**: Effective communication is the foundation of strong human relations skills. It involves the ability to convey information clearly and concisely, listen actively, and understand non-verbal cues. Effective communication fosters transparency, builds trust, and enhances collaboration. Managers who communicate well can articulate the organization's goals and expectations, provide constructive feedback, and resolve misunderstandings. They also create an open and inclusive environment where employees feel comfortable sharing their ideas and concerns.

- **Empathy**: Empathy is the ability to understand and share the feelings of others. It involves putting oneself in another's shoes and seeing the situation from their perspective. Empathetic managers can build strong relationships with their team members, foster a supportive work environment, and improve employee satisfaction and retention. Empathy helps managers understand the needs, concerns, and motivations of their team members, enabling them to provide better support and guidance. It also enhances communication, as employees feel heard and understood.

- **Conflict Resolution**: Conflict resolution involves the ability to address and resolve disagreements in a constructive manner. It requires good communication, negotiation, and problem-solving skills. Managers who excel in conflict resolution can identify the underlying causes of conflict, facilitate open dialogue, and find mutually acceptable solutions. They create a positive work environment where conflicts are seen as opportunities for growth and improvement rather than obstacles. Effective conflict resolution enhances team cohesion, productivity, and morale.

- **Teamwork**: Teamwork involves the ability to work collaboratively with others towards a common goal. It requires good communication, cooperation, and coordination. Managers who foster teamwork can build strong, cohesive teams that are more productive and innovative. They create an inclusive environment where everyone feels valued and motivated to contribute to the team's success. Effective teamwork enhances problem-solving, creativity, and employee satisfaction.

- **Motivation**: Motivation involves the ability to inspire and encourage others to perform at their best. It requires an understanding of what drives individual team members and the ability to create a supportive and engaging work environment. Managers who excel in motivation can identify and leverage the strengths of their team members, provide opportunities for growth and development, and recognize and reward achievements. They create a positive work environment that fosters employee engagement, satisfaction, and retention.

3. Practical Tips for Enhancing Human Relations Skills through Practice and Feedback

➢ **Enhancing Communication Skills**:

- **Active Listening**: Focus on listening to understand rather than to respond. Pay attention to the speaker, maintain eye contact, and avoid interrupting. Reflect what you've heard to ensure understanding.
- **Clear and Concise Communication**: Be clear and concise in your communication. Avoid jargon and complex language. Use simple and direct language to convey your message.
- **Non-verbal Communication**: Be aware of your body language, facial expressions, and tone of voice. These non-verbal cues can convey a lot of information and affect how your message is received.
- **Provide Feedback**: Give and receive feedback constructively. Focus on specific behaviors and provide suggestions for improvement. Encourage open dialogue and be open to receiving feedback from others.

➢ **Enhancing Empathy**:

- **Active Listening**: Listen actively and attentively to understand the speaker's perspective and feelings. Show empathy by acknowledging their emotions and validating their experiences.
- **Ask Questions**: Ask open-ended questions to gain a deeper understanding of the speaker's perspective. Show genuine interest and curiosity in their experiences and feelings.
- **Practice Perspective-Taking**: Put yourself in the other person's shoes and try to see the situation from their perspective. Consider how they might be feeling and what they might be thinking.
- **Show Compassion**: Show compassion and understanding towards others. Offer support and help when needed. Express empathy through your words and actions.

➢ **Enhancing Conflict Resolution Skills**:

- **Identify the Underlying Causes**: Identify the underlying causes of the conflict and address them directly. Focus on the issues rather than the personalities involved.

- **Facilitate Open Dialogue**: Encourage open and honest communication between the parties involved. Create a safe space where everyone feels comfortable expressing their views and concerns.
- **Find Mutually Acceptable Solutions**: Work towards finding mutually acceptable solutions that address the concerns of all parties involved. Focus on win-win solutions that benefit everyone.
- **Be Fair and Consistent**: Be fair and consistent in your approach to conflict resolution. Avoid taking sides and treat everyone involved with respect and fairness.

➢ **D. Enhancing Teamwork Skills**:

- **Encourage Collaboration**: Encourage collaboration and teamwork by creating opportunities for team members to work together on projects and tasks. Foster a collaborative culture where everyone feels valued and motivated to contribute.
- **Recognize and Leverage Strengths**: Recognize and leverage the strengths of each team member. Assign tasks and responsibilities based on individual strengths and skills.
- **Promote Inclusivity**: Promote inclusivity by creating an environment where everyone feels valued and included. Encourage diversity of thought and ideas.
- **Foster Open Communication**: Foster open and transparent communication within the team. Encourage team members to share their ideas, concerns, and feedback openly and honestly.

➢ **E. Enhancing Motivation Skills**:

- **Understand Individual Motivations**: Understand what motivates each team member and tailor your approach accordingly. Consider individual needs, preferences, and goals.
- **Provide Opportunities for Growth**: Provide opportunities for growth and development. Encourage continuous learning and development through training, mentorship, and career development programs.

- **Recognize and Reward Achievements**: Recognize and reward achievements and contributions. Celebrate successes and milestones and provide positive reinforcement.
- **Create a Supportive Work Environment**: Create a supportive work environment where team members feel valued, respected, and supported. Encourage work-life balance and provide support and resources to help team members succeed.

In conclusion, human relations skills are essential for effective management and leadership. By developing and enhancing these skills, managers can create a positive work environment, build strong teams, and achieve organizational goals. Through practice and feedback, managers can continuously improve their human relations skills and become more effective leaders.

Case Study: Improving Team Dynamics at Tech Innovators Inc.

Background:

Tech Innovators Inc. is a mid-sized technology company specializing in software development. The company has experienced rapid growth over the past five years, resulting in a diverse workforce composed of individuals from various cultural backgrounds and professional experiences. The management team, led by Sarah Thompson, has recognized the importance of fostering a positive work environment and enhancing team collaboration to maintain high productivity and innovation levels.

Despite the company's success, several issues have emerged within the team:

1. **Communication Breakdown:** There have been instances of miscommunication between team members, leading to project delays and frustration.
2. **Lack of Trust:** Some employees feel hesitant to voice their ideas and concerns due to a lack of trust in the team.
3. **Conflicts:** Conflicts between team members have become more frequent, affecting the overall morale and productivity.

4. **Poor Teamwork:** The team struggles to work cohesively, with individuals often working in silos rather than collaborating.
5. **Low Motivation:** Employee engagement and motivation have decreased, leading to lower performance and higher turnover rates.

Strategy to Solve Problems:

1. Enhancing Communication:

- **Workshops on Effective Communication:** Conduct workshops focused on improving communication skills, including active listening, clear and concise messaging, and understanding non-verbal cues.
- **Regular Team Meetings:** Establish regular team meetings to ensure everyone is on the same page and to facilitate open dialogue.
- **Feedback Mechanisms:** Implement a structured feedback system where team members can give and receive constructive feedback regularly.

2. Building Trust and Relationships:

- **Team-Building Activities:** Organize team-building activities that encourage interaction and relationship-building outside the regular work environment.
- **Transparency in Decision-Making:** Increase transparency in the decision-making process to build trust. Share information about company goals, challenges, and successes with the team.
- **Mentorship Programs:** Pair team members with mentors to foster personal and professional development and build trust through one-on-one interactions.

3. Resolving Conflicts:

- **Conflict Resolution Training:** Provide training on conflict resolution techniques, including negotiation, mediation, and problem-solving.

- **Open Door Policy:** Encourage an open-door policy where employees feel comfortable discussing their issues with management.
- **Mediation Sessions:** When conflicts arise, hold mediation sessions facilitated by a neutral third party to address and resolve issues constructively.

4. Enhancing Teamwork:

- **Collaborative Projects:** Assign projects that require collaboration and interdependence among team members.
- **Strength-Based Assignments:** Identify and leverage the strengths of each team member by assigning tasks that align with their skills and expertise.
- **Inclusivity Initiatives:** Promote an inclusive work environment by encouraging diversity of thought and creating opportunities for all team members to contribute.

5. Motivating and Engaging Employees:

- **Recognition and Rewards:** Implement a recognition and rewards program to celebrate achievements and contributions.
- **Professional Development:** Provide opportunities for professional development through training, workshops, and career advancement programs.
- **Supportive Work Environment:** Foster a supportive work environment that encourages work-life balance, provides necessary resources, and supports employees' well-being.

Implementation: Sarah Thompson and her management team decided to roll out the strategy over six months:

1. **Month 1-2:** Focus on communication workshops and establishing regular team meetings. Implement the feedback system.
2. **Month 3:** Organize team-building activities and launch mentorship programs.
3. **Month 4:** Conduct conflict resolution training and introduce the open-door policy.

4. **Month 5:** Start collaborative projects and assign tasks based on team members' strengths.
5. **Month 6:** Roll out the recognition and rewards program and provide professional development opportunities.

Outcome: After six months, the management team observed significant improvements:

- **Enhanced Communication:** Miscommunications decreased, leading to smoother project execution.
- **Increased Trust:** Team members were more willing to share ideas and feedback, resulting in innovative solutions.
- **Resolved Conflicts:** The frequency and intensity of conflicts reduced, and team morale improved.
- **Improved Teamwork:** Collaboration and teamwork increased, with team members supporting each other more effectively.
- **Higher Motivation:** Employee engagement and motivation levels rose, leading to better performance and lower turnover rates.

Tech Innovators Inc. saw a positive transformation in its work environment, thanks to the focused efforts on improving human relations skills. The company continued to build on these improvements, ensuring sustained success and a happy, productive workforce.

Question Bank:

2 Marks:

1. Define human relations skills and explain their importance in the workplace.

2. What is the role of communication in enhancing managerial effectiveness?

3. How does building trust and relationships impact team performance?

4. What are the key components of effective conflict resolution?

5. How can managers foster teamwork and collaboration within their teams?

5 Marks:

1. Explain the significance of human relations skills in managerial roles. Discuss how these skills contribute to achieving organizational goals.

2. Analyze the importance of effective communication for managers. Provide examples of how good communication can prevent misunderstandings and build trust within a team.

3. Describe the ways in which managers can build and maintain trust with their team members. Discuss the impact of trust on team dynamics and performance.

4. Discuss the strategies managers can use to resolve conflicts within their teams. Provide examples of how conflict resolution can improve team morale and productivity.

5. Examine the role of teamwork in enhancing productivity and innovation. Discuss how managers can create an inclusive environment that fosters collaboration and leverages individual strengths.

6. How can technology be utilized to overcome communication barriers in organizations? Provide examples.

10 Marks:

1. Discuss the importance of motivation in employee performance and satisfaction. How can managers tailor their management style to meet the individual needs of their team members?

2. Explain how managers can promote a positive organizational culture. Discuss the behaviors, attitudes, and values that contribute to a positive work environment.

3. Analyze the key components of human relations skills: communication, empathy, conflict resolution, teamwork, and motivation. Discuss how each component contributes to effective management.

4. Provide practical tips for enhancing human relations skills through practice and feedback. Discuss specific techniques for improving communication, empathy, conflict resolution, teamwork, and motivation.

5. Reflect on the statement: "Human relations skills are essential for effective management and leadership." Discuss how managers can continuously improve these skills to become more effective leader

Module 3

Conceptual Skills

1. Definition of Conceptual Skills:

Conceptual skills refer to the ability to understand complex situations, think abstractly, and see the big picture. These skills involve recognizing patterns, understanding relationships between different elements, and making connections that are not immediately obvious. In the context of strategic management and decision-making, conceptual skills enable managers to envision the future, develop long-term plans, and make decisions that align with the organization's goals and objectives.

Examples of Conceptual Skills in Strategic Management and Decision-Making:

- **Strategic Planning**: Strategic planning involves setting long-term goals, identifying the necessary steps to achieve these goals, and allocating resources accordingly. For example, a CEO of a technology company may use conceptual skills to identify emerging market trends, predict future technological advancements, and develop a strategic plan to position the company as a market leader. This involves analyzing internal capabilities, assessing external opportunities and threats, and making informed decisions about where to invest resources.
- **Problem Solving**: Conceptual skills are crucial for solving complex problems that require a deep understanding of the underlying issues and the ability to generate innovative solutions. For example, a manager in a manufacturing company may need to address a decline in production efficiency. Using conceptual skills, the manager can analyze the entire production process, identify bottlenecks, and develop a comprehensive plan to improve efficiency, such as implementing new technologies or reorganizing the workflow.
- **Decision-Making**: Effective decision-making requires the ability to evaluate multiple options, consider the long-term implications of each choice, and make decisions that align with

the organization's strategic goals. For example, a marketing manager may need to decide between investing in a new advertising campaign or launching a new product line. Using conceptual skills, the manager can assess the potential impact of each option on the company's brand, market position, and revenue, and make an informed decision that supports the overall strategy.

- **Innovation and Creativity**: Conceptual skills enable managers to think creatively and develop innovative solutions to challenges. For example, a product development manager may use conceptual skills to envision a new product that meets unmet customer needs, differentiates the company from competitors, and drives growth. This involves thinking outside the box, challenging assumptions, and exploring new ideas and possibilities.

- **Visionary Leadership**: Visionary leadership involves the ability to create and communicate a compelling vision for the future, inspire and motivate employees, and guide the organization towards achieving this vision. For example, a CEO may use conceptual skills to articulate a vision of becoming a global leader in sustainability, develop a strategic plan to achieve this vision, and inspire employees to embrace sustainable practices and innovate new solutions.

- **Systems Thinking**: Systems thinking involves understanding the interconnectedness of different elements within an organization and how changes in one area can impact others. For example, a supply chain manager may use systems thinking to understand how changes in supplier relationships, production processes, and distribution networks affect overall supply chain performance. This enables the manager to make informed decisions that optimize the entire supply chain, rather than focusing on individual components.

2. How Conceptual Skills Differ at Different Managerial Levels:

Conceptual skills are essential at all levels of management, but their importance and application vary depending on the managerial level. Understanding these differences is crucial for developing effective managers who can contribute to the organization's success at every level.

Front-Line Managers: Front-line managers, also known as first-line managers or supervisors, are responsible for overseeing the day-to-day operations of a specific team or department. At this level, conceptual skills are important but are often focused on understanding and improving operational processes.

- **Process Improvement**: Front-line managers use conceptual skills to identify inefficiencies and develop solutions to improve processes. For example, a front-line manager in a retail store may analyze customer service processes to identify bottlenecks and implement changes to reduce wait times and improve customer satisfaction.
- **Short-Term Planning**: While front-line managers primarily focus on short-term goals, they still need to consider how their actions align with the organization's overall strategy. For example, a production supervisor may develop a weekly production schedule that aligns with the company's long-term goal of reducing inventory costs.
- **Problem Solving**: Front-line managers frequently encounter operational problems that require quick and effective solutions. For example, a restaurant manager may need to address staffing shortages or equipment malfunctions by analyzing the situation, identifying potential solutions, and implementing the best course of action.

Middle Managers: Middle managers bridge the gap between front-line managers and top executives. They are responsible for translating the organization's strategic goals into actionable plans and coordinating the efforts of different departments.

- **Departmental Coordination**: Middle managers use conceptual skills to understand how different departments interrelate and how changes in one area can impact others. For example, a marketing manager may need to coordinate with the sales and product development teams to ensure that marketing campaigns align with sales goals and product launch timelines.
- **Strategic Implementation**: Middle managers play a key role in implementing the organization's strategic plans. For example, an operations manager may develop and execute a plan to

increase production capacity in response to growing demand, ensuring that the plan aligns with the company's long-term goals.

- **Change Management**: Middle managers are often responsible for leading change initiatives within their departments. For example, an HR manager may implement a new performance management system, requiring an understanding of how the change will impact employees and the organization's culture.

Top Managers: Top managers, also known as executives or senior leaders, are responsible for setting the organization's overall direction and making high-level strategic decisions.

- **Vision and Strategy**: Top managers use conceptual skills to develop and communicate a clear vision for the organization's future. For example, a CEO may articulate a vision of expanding into new international markets and develop a strategic plan to achieve this goal.
- **Long-Term Planning**: Top managers focus on long-term goals and ensure that the organization's resources are allocated effectively to achieve these goals. For example, a CFO may develop a long-term financial strategy that includes investment in new technologies and cost-saving initiatives.
- **Risk Management**: Top managers need to identify and mitigate potential risks that could impact the organization's success. For example, a risk manager may analyze market trends, regulatory changes, and competitive pressures to identify potential risks and develop strategies to address them.
- **Corporate Governance**: Top managers are responsible for ensuring that the organization adheres to ethical standards and regulatory requirements. For example, a board of directors may establish policies and procedures to ensure transparency, accountability, and compliance with legal and ethical standards.

3. Techniques for Improving Strategic Thinking and Long-Term Planning Abilities

Improving strategic thinking and long-term planning abilities is essential for managers at all levels. These skills enable managers to develop and implement effective strategies that drive organizational success. Here are some techniques for enhancing these abilities:

- ❖ **Continuous Learning**:

- **Stay Informed**: Keep up-to-date with industry trends, market developments, and technological advancements. This helps managers understand the external environment and identify opportunities and threats.
- **Professional Development**: Participate in training programs, workshops, and conferences to enhance strategic thinking skills. For example, attending a leadership development program can provide valuable insights and tools for strategic planning.

- ❖ **Systems Thinking**:

- **Understand Interconnections**: Develop the ability to see the organization as a system of interconnected parts. This helps managers understand how changes in one area can impact others and make informed decisions.
- **Scenario Planning**: Use scenario planning to explore different future scenarios and their potential impact on the organization. This helps managers develop flexible strategies that can adapt to changing circumstances.

- ❖ **Analytical Thinking**:

- **Data Analysis**: Use data analysis to make informed decisions. Analyze internal and external data to identify trends, patterns, and insights that can inform strategic planning.
- **SWOT Analysis**: Conduct SWOT (Strengths, Weaknesses, Opportunities, Threats) analysis to assess the organization's internal capabilities and external environment. This helps managers identify areas for improvement and opportunities for growth.

- ❖ **Creative Thinking**:

- **Brainstorming**: Encourage brainstorming sessions to generate innovative ideas and solutions. This helps managers think outside the box and explore new possibilities.
- **Design Thinking**: Use design thinking principles to develop creative solutions to complex problems. This involves empathizing with users, defining the problem, ideating solutions, prototyping, and testing.

❖ **Long-Term Visioning:**

- **Vision Statements**: Develop and communicate a clear vision statement that outlines the organization's long-term goals and aspirations. This provides direction and inspires employees to work towards the vision.
- **Backcasting**: Use backcasting to develop long-term plans by envisioning a desired future state and working backward to identify the steps needed to achieve it.

❖ **Collaborative Planning:**

- **Cross-Functional Teams**: Involve cross-functional teams in the strategic planning process. This brings diverse perspectives and expertise to the table, enhancing the quality of strategic decisions.
- **Stakeholder Engagement**: Engage stakeholders in the planning process to ensure their needs and expectations are considered. This helps build support and alignment for the organization's strategy.

❖ **Strategic Execution:**

- **Action Plans**: Develop detailed action plans that outline the steps needed to implement the organization's strategy. This includes setting goals, assigning responsibilities, and establishing timelines.
- **Performance Metrics**: Establish performance metrics to track progress and measure the success of strategic initiatives. This helps managers identify areas for improvement and make data-driven decisions.

❖ **Reflective Practice**:

- **Regular Reviews**: Conduct regular reviews of the organization's strategy and performance. This helps managers assess progress, identify challenges, and make necessary adjustments.
- **Lessons Learned**: Reflect on past experiences and learn from successes and failures. This helps managers develop a deeper understanding of what works and what doesn't, informing future strategic decisions.

Thus, conceptual skills are essential for effective strategic management and decision-making. By developing and enhancing these skills, managers at all levels can contribute to the organization's long-term success. Through continuous learning, systems thinking, analytical thinking, creative thinking, long-term visioning, collaborative planning, strategic execution, and reflective practice, managers can improve their strategic thinking and long-term planning abilities and become more effective leaders.

Case Study: Enhancing Conceptual Skills at TechFuture Inc.

Background:

TechFuture Inc., a mid-sized technology company, specializes in software development and IT consulting. Over the past decade, the company has experienced rapid growth, positioning itself as a key player in the technology industry. TechFuture's success is driven by its ability to innovate and stay ahead of market trends, but with growth comes new challenges. As the company expands, the leadership team recognizes the need to strengthen their conceptual skills to maintain their competitive edge and achieve long-term success.

Scenario: Despite its growth and market position, TechFuture faces several critical issues that threaten its long-term success:

1. **Production Efficiency Decline**:
   - ○ **Problem**: John Doe, a middle manager in the manufacturing department, notices a significant decline

in production efficiency. The outdated equipment and poorly organized workflow contribute to bottlenecks, resulting in delays and increased costs.
- **Impact**: The inefficiencies affect the overall product quality, customer satisfaction, and operational costs, jeopardizing the company's competitive position.

2. **Strategic Decision-Making Challenges**:
   - **Problem**: Sarah Johnson, the marketing manager, struggles with making strategic decisions that align with TechFuture's long-term goals. Faced with choosing between a new advertising campaign or launching a new product line, she finds it challenging to evaluate the long-term implications of each option.
   - **Impact**: Poor decision-making could lead to misallocation of resources, missed market opportunities, and potential revenue loss.

3. **Innovation Stagnation**:
   - **Problem**: Mark Lee, the product development manager, recognizes that the company's innovation efforts have plateaued. The team is struggling to generate new ideas that meet unmet customer needs and differentiate TechFuture from competitors.
   - **Impact**: Innovation stagnation threatens TechFuture's market leadership and growth prospects.

4. **Lack of Visionary Leadership**:
   - **Problem**: While Jane Smith, the CEO, has a vision for TechFuture's future, communicating this vision and inspiring employees to work towards it is challenging. There is a disconnect between the strategic vision and the employees' day-to-day activities.
   - **Impact**: Without clear and compelling visionary leadership, employees lack motivation and direction, which could result in decreased productivity and alignment with the company's goals.

5. **Supply Chain Disruptions**:
   - **Problem**: Lisa Brown, the supply chain manager, faces disruptions due to changes in supplier relationships and production processes. Understanding the interconnectedness of these elements and their impact on the overall supply chain performance is complex.

- o **Impact**: Supply chain disruptions lead to delays, increased costs, and potential loss of customer trust.

Strategies for Improvement: To address these issues, TechFuture's leadership team implements several strategies to enhance their conceptual skills and drive long-term success:

1. **Improving Production Efficiency**:
   - o **Solution**: John Doe implements new technologies and reorganizes the workflow to address production inefficiencies. By adopting lean manufacturing principles and investing in modern equipment, TechFuture can streamline operations and reduce bottlenecks.
   - o **Outcome**: Enhanced production efficiency leads to improved product quality, reduced operational costs, and increased customer satisfaction.
2. **Enhancing Strategic Decision-Making**:
   - o **Solution**: Sarah Johnson uses data analysis and SWOT analysis to evaluate the potential impact of each strategic option. By leveraging data-driven insights and considering long-term implications, she can make informed decisions that align with TechFuture's strategic goals.
   - o **Outcome**: Improved decision-making ensures effective resource allocation, maximizes market opportunities, and supports revenue growth.
3. **Revitalizing Innovation**:
   - o **Solution**: Mark Lee fosters a culture of creativity and innovation within the product development team. By encouraging brainstorming sessions and employing design thinking principles, the team can generate new ideas and develop innovative solutions.
   - o **Outcome**: Revitalized innovation efforts result in groundbreaking products that meet customer needs, differentiate TechFuture from competitors, and drive growth.
4. **Strengthening Visionary Leadership**:
   - o **Solution**: Jane Smith develops a clear and compelling vision statement that outlines TechFuture's long-term

goals and aspirations. She communicates this vision regularly and aligns it with employees' day-to-day activities through transparent leadership and motivational initiatives.

- o **Outcome**: Enhanced visionary leadership inspires and motivates employees, fostering a sense of purpose and direction that drives productivity and alignment with the company's goals.

5. **Optimizing Supply Chain Management**:
   - o **Solution**: Lisa Brown adopts systems thinking to understand the interconnectedness of different elements within the supply chain. She implements scenario planning to anticipate potential disruptions and develop flexible strategies to mitigate risks.
   - o **Outcome**: Optimized supply chain management ensures smooth operations, reduces costs, and maintains customer trust and satisfaction.

TechFuture Inc. exemplifies the importance of conceptual skills in strategic management and decision-making. By addressing the issues of production efficiency, strategic decision-making, innovation stagnation, visionary leadership, and supply chain disruptions, the company can strengthen its market position and achieve long-term success. Through continuous learning, systems thinking, analytical thinking, creative thinking, long-term visioning, collaborative planning, strategic execution, and reflective practice, TechFuture's leadership team can improve their conceptual skills and lead the company towards a prosperous future.

Question Bank:

2 Marks:

1. Define conceptual skills and explain their significance in strategic management.?

2. How do conceptual skills aid in strategic planning.

3. What role do conceptual skills play in problem-solving and decision-making.

4. Explain the importance of systems thinking for managers?

5. Describe how conceptual skills differ at different managerial levels.

5 Marks:

1. How can brainstorming sessions enhance a manager's creative thinking?

2. What are conceptual skills and why are they important for managers?

3. What is systems thinking and how does it benefit a supply chain manager?

4. Give an example of how a middle manager might use conceptual skills in departmental coordination.

5. How do conceptual skills differ between front-line managers and top managers?

10 Marks:

1. Compare and contrast the use of conceptual skills in problem-solving at the front-line management level versus the top management level. Provide examples to illustrate your points.

2. Explain the importance of continuous learning in improving strategic thinking and long-term planning abilities. Provide specific techniques managers can use for continuous learning.

3. Describe the process of scenario planning and how it can help managers develop flexible strategies. Include an example of a scenario planning exercise in a manufacturing company.

4. Discuss the role of conceptual skills in strategic planning and provide an example of how a CEO might use these skills to position their company as a market leader.

5. How can cross-functional teams and stakeholder engagement improve the quality of strategic decisions? Provide an example of a collaborative planning process in an organization.

Module 4:

Technical Skills

1.Definition: Technical skills refer to the specific knowledge and abilities required to perform tasks related to a particular field or profession. These skills involve the practical application of theoretical knowledge and are essential for executing job-specific duties effectively. Technical skills are often gained through education, training, and hands-on experience. In the context of managerial roles, technical skills are crucial for understanding the technical aspects of the work being done, guiding teams, and making informed decisions.

Examples of Technical Skills Relevant to Different Functional Areas:

Marketing:

- **Market Research**: Understanding market research techniques and tools is critical for gathering and analyzing data about consumer preferences, market trends, and competitive landscape. Proficiency in tools such as Google Analytics, SPSS, and survey software is essential for making data-driven marketing decisions.
- **Digital Marketing**: In the digital age, technical skills in SEO (Search Engine Optimization), SEM (Search Engine Marketing), content management systems, social media marketing, and email marketing platforms like MailChimp are indispensable for reaching and engaging with customers online.
- **Data Analysis**: Ability to analyze marketing data to measure the effectiveness of campaigns, understand customer behavior, and make strategic decisions. Tools like Excel, Tableau, and various CRM (Customer Relationship Management) systems are crucial.

Finance:

- **Financial Analysis**: Skills in analyzing financial statements, understanding financial ratios, and interpreting financial data are fundamental. Knowledge of tools like Excel, QuickBooks, and financial modeling software is essential.

- **Budgeting and Forecasting**: Proficiency in creating budgets and financial forecasts to plan for future financial performance. This includes using software like SAP, Oracle Financials, and specialized budgeting tools.
- **Investment Analysis**: Understanding investment principles, risk assessment, and portfolio management. Skills in using Bloomberg terminals, stock analysis software, and various financial databases are critical.

Operations:

- **Process Improvement**: Knowledge of methodologies like Lean, Six Sigma, and Total Quality Management (TQM) to enhance efficiency and quality in operational processes. Familiarity with tools like Minitab for statistical analysis is important.
- **Supply Chain Management**: Skills in managing the flow of goods and services, including logistics, inventory management, and procurement. Proficiency in ERP (Enterprise Resource Planning) systems like SAP and Oracle is crucial.
- **Project Management**: Ability to plan, execute, and oversee projects to ensure they are completed on time and within budget. This involves using project management software such as Microsoft Project, Asana, and Jira.

Human Resources:

- **Talent Management**: Skills in recruiting, training, and developing employees. Familiarity with HR software like Workday, BambooHR, and LinkedIn Recruiter is essential.
- **Compensation and Benefits**: Knowledge of designing and managing compensation structures and employee benefits programs. Proficiency in payroll software and benefits administration platforms is important.
- **Employee Relations**: Skills in handling employee relations, conflict resolution, and compliance with labor laws. Understanding of HR analytics tools to analyze employee data and improve HR practices.

Information Technology:

- **Software Development**: Proficiency in programming languages (e.g., Java, Python, C++), software development methodologies (e.g., Agile, Scrum), and development tools (e.g., Git, JIRA).
- **Network Administration**: Skills in managing and maintaining computer networks, understanding network protocols, and using network management tools like Cisco, Wireshark, and SolarWinds.
- **Cybersecurity**: Knowledge of cybersecurity principles, risk management, and proficiency in using security tools like firewalls, intrusion detection systems (IDS), and security information and event management (SIEM) systems.

2.Importance of Technical Skills at Various Managerial Levels

Technical skills are vital across all managerial levels, though their importance and application may vary depending on the specific role and responsibilities of the manager.

Front-Line Managers:

Front-line managers, also known as first-line managers or supervisors, directly oversee the work of individual contributors and are responsible for ensuring that daily operations run smoothly. At this level, technical skills are essential for:

1. Direct Supervision: Front-line managers need to understand the technical aspects of the tasks their team members are performing to provide effective guidance, support, and problem-solving assistance. For example, a front-line manager in a manufacturing plant must understand the machinery and production processes to troubleshoot issues and ensure quality standards are met.

2. Training and Development: Front-line managers are often responsible for training new employees and ensuring that team members are proficient in their roles. This requires a deep understanding of the technical skills and processes involved. For instance, a front-line manager in a call center needs to be proficient in the customer service software and call handling techniques to train new hires effectively.

3. Performance Evaluation: To accurately assess and improve employee performance, front-line managers must have a solid grasp of the technical skills required for the job. This enables them to provide constructive feedback and identify areas for improvement. For example, a front-line manager in a retail setting must understand sales techniques and point-of-sale systems to evaluate and enhance employee performance.

Middle Managers:

Middle managers act as a bridge between front-line managers and top executives. They are responsible for implementing organizational strategies and ensuring that departmental goals are achieved. At this level, technical skills are important for:

1. Strategic Implementation: Middle managers need to understand the technical details of their department's operations to effectively translate organizational strategies into actionable plans. For example, a middle manager in the IT department must understand the technical requirements of a new software implementation to plan and execute the project successfully.

2. Cross-Functional Coordination: Middle managers often work with other departments to achieve common goals. Technical skills enable them to communicate effectively with colleagues from different functional areas and coordinate efforts. For instance, a middle manager in marketing needs to understand the technical aspects of product development to collaborate effectively with the R&D team.

3. Resource Management: Middle managers are responsible for managing resources, including personnel, budget, and technology. Technical skills help them make informed decisions about resource allocation and utilization. For example, a middle manager in finance must understand the technical details of financial analysis to allocate budget effectively and monitor financial performance.

Top Managers:

Top managers, including executives and senior leaders, are responsible for setting the organization's overall direction and making high-level strategic decisions. While top managers may not need to possess the same level of technical expertise as front-line and middle managers, technical skills are still important for:

1. Strategic Decision-Making: Top managers need a broad understanding of the technical aspects of their industry to make informed strategic decisions. For example, a CEO of a tech company must understand the latest technological trends and innovations to set the company's strategic direction and make investment decisions.

2. Innovation and Growth: Top managers must identify opportunities for innovation and growth. Technical skills enable them to understand the potential impact of new technologies and processes on the organization. For instance, a CFO must understand the technical aspects of financial technologies (fintech) to explore opportunities for improving financial operations and services.

3. Leadership and Vision: Top managers need to articulate a clear vision for the organization and inspire employees to work towards it. Technical skills help them understand the capabilities and limitations of their organization's technology and processes, allowing them to set realistic and achievable goals. For example, a COO must understand the technical details of operations to develop a vision for operational excellence and efficiency.

3. How to Develop and Maintain Technical Expertise in a Rapidly Changing Environment

In today's fast-paced and constantly evolving business landscape, developing and maintaining technical expertise is crucial for staying competitive and achieving long-term success. Here are several strategies for enhancing and sustaining technical skills:

1. Continuous Learning:

- **Formal Education**: Pursue advanced degrees, certifications, and professional development courses to deepen your technical knowledge and stay current with industry trends. Many universities and professional organizations offer online courses and certifications in various technical fields.
- **Workshops and Seminars**: Attend workshops, seminars, and conferences to learn from industry experts, gain new insights, and network with professionals. These events provide opportunities to stay updated on the latest advancements and best practices in your field.

2. Hands-On Experience:

- **Practical Application**: Apply your technical skills in real-world situations to gain practical experience. This could involve taking on challenging projects, experimenting with new technologies, and solving complex problems.
- **Cross-Training**: Engage in cross-training opportunities to learn new skills from different departments or functional areas. This broadens your technical expertise and enhances your ability to collaborate effectively with colleagues.

3. Staying Updated with Industry Trends:

- **Industry Publications**: Subscribe to industry journals, magazines, and newsletters to stay informed about the latest developments, research, and innovations. Reading industry publications regularly helps you stay ahead of trends and understand the evolving landscape.
- **Online Resources**: Utilize online resources such as webinars, podcasts, and blogs to access valuable information and insights. Many industry experts share their knowledge and experiences through these platforms, providing valuable learning opportunities.

4. Networking and Collaboration:

- **Professional Associations**: Join professional associations and organizations related to your field. These groups offer networking opportunities, resources, and events that can help you stay connected with industry peers and experts.

- **Mentorship and Coaching**: Seek mentorship and coaching from experienced professionals who can provide guidance, support, and insights. Mentors can help you navigate your career path, develop your technical skills, and achieve your professional goals.

5. Leveraging Technology:

- **Online Learning Platforms**: Take advantage of online learning platforms such as Coursera, Udacity, LinkedIn Learning, and edX to access a wide range of courses and tutorials. These platforms offer flexible learning options that allow you to learn at your own pace.
- **Software and Tools**: Familiarize yourself with the latest software, tools, and technologies relevant to your field. Practicing with these tools helps you stay proficient and adaptable to new technological advancements.

6. Reflective Practice:

- **Self-Assessment**: Regularly assess your technical skills and identify areas for improvement. Self-assessment tools and feedback from colleagues can help you recognize your strengths and weaknesses.
- **Continuous Improvement**: Adopt a mindset of continuous improvement by setting personal and professional development goals. Regularly update your skills and knowledge to stay competitive and effective in your role.

7. Organizational Support:

- **Training Programs**: Advocate for and participate in company-sponsored training programs and workshops. Organizations that invest in employee development often provide opportunities for technical skill enhancement.

- **Knowledge Sharing**: Encourage a culture of knowledge sharing within your organization. Collaborate with colleagues to share best practices, insights, and technical expertise.

8. Adaptability and Flexibility:

- **Embrace Change**: Stay open to new ideas, technologies, and methodologies. Embracing change and being adaptable helps you stay relevant and effective in a rapidly evolving environment.
- **Lifelong Learning**: Commit to lifelong learning and professional growth. Recognize that the journey of developing and maintaining technical expertise is ongoing and requires continuous effort.

In conclusion, technical skills are essential for managers at all levels and across various functional areas. Developing and maintaining technical expertise in a rapidly changing environment requires continuous learning, hands-on experience, staying updated with industry trends, networking and collaboration, leveraging technology, reflective practice, organizational support, and adaptability. By adopting these strategies, managers can enhance their technical skills, stay competitive, and contribute effectively to their organization's success.

Case Study: Enhancing Technical Skills at Innovate Marketing Solutions

Background:

Innovate Marketing Solutions (IMS) is a mid-sized marketing agency specializing in digital marketing, market research, and branding. The agency has seen substantial growth in recent years, resulting in a larger and more diverse team. Despite the growth, the company faced challenges related to the rapidly evolving digital landscape, with new tools, platforms, and strategies emerging frequently.

Issues Faced:

1. **Outdated Technical Skills:** Team members used outdated tools and techniques, leading to inefficiencies and suboptimal results.

2. **Lack of Technical Training:** There was no structured training program to keep employees updated with the latest trends and technologies.
3. **Ineffective Data Analysis:** The team struggled with analyzing marketing data effectively, impacting their ability to make data-driven decisions.
4. **Poor Cross-Functional Collaboration:** A lack of understanding of technical processes in different departments led to communication breakdowns and project delays.
5. **Limited Use of Advanced Tools:** Advanced tools and software were underutilized due to inadequate training.

Strategy to Solve Problems:

1. Continuous Learning:

- **Formal Education and Certifications:** Partner with online learning platforms like Coursera and LinkedIn Learning to offer courses and certifications in digital marketing, data analysis, and emerging technologies.
- **Workshops and Seminars:** Host quarterly workshops and seminars led by industry experts to provide hands-on training and insights into the latest marketing trends and tools.

2. Hands-On Experience:

- **Practical Application:** Implement a project-based learning approach where employees work on real-world projects using new tools and techniques.
- **Cross-Training:** Facilitate cross-departmental training sessions to broaden technical expertise and enhance collaboration.

3. Staying Updated with Industry Trends:

- **Industry Publications:** Subscribe to leading marketing journals, blogs, and newsletters. Create a shared resource library for employees.
- **Online Resources:** Organize regular webinars and podcasts with industry experts to discuss the latest trends and advancements.

4. Networking and Collaboration:

- **Professional Associations:** Encourage employees to join professional marketing associations and attend networking events and conferences.
- **Mentorship and Coaching:** Establish a mentorship program where experienced employees guide colleagues in developing technical skills.

5. Leveraging Technology:

- **Online Learning Platforms:** Provide access to platforms like Udacity and edX for continuous learning and skill development.
- **Software and Tools:** Invest in training for advanced marketing tools such as Tableau for data visualization, HubSpot for marketing automation, and Google Analytics for web analytics.

6. Reflective Practice:

- **Self-Assessment:** Implement regular self-assessment and peer review sessions to identify strengths and areas for improvement.
- **Continuous Improvement:** Set personal and team development goals to ensure ongoing improvement and adaptation to new technologies.

7. Organizational Support:

- **Training Programs:** Develop comprehensive training programs covering the latest tools, data analysis techniques, and digital strategies.
- **Knowledge Sharing:** Create a platform for employees to share tutorials, success stories, and best practices related to new tools and techniques.

8. Adaptability and Flexibility:

- **Embrace Change:** Foster a culture that encourages experimentation and adaptation to new technologies and methods.
- **Lifelong Learning:** Promote a mindset of lifelong learning and professional development through regular communication about the importance of staying current with industry advancements.

Implementation:

IMS implemented the strategy over six months, focusing on formal education, practical application, industry updates, networking, technology training, reflective practice, organizational support, and adaptability.

Outcome:

After six months, IMS saw significant improvements:

- **Updated Technical Skills:** Employees became proficient with the latest tools and techniques, leading to more efficient and effective campaigns.
- **Structured Technical Training:** New training programs ensured employees stayed current with industry trends and technologies.
- **Effective Data Analysis:** Improved data analysis skills led to better decision-making and more successful marketing strategies.
- **Enhanced Cross-Functional Collaboration:** Improved understanding of technical processes across departments enhanced communication and project outcomes.
- **Increased Utilization of Advanced Tools:** Effective use of advanced tools enhanced productivity and campaign results.

IMS successfully addressed technical skill gaps, resulting in a more competent, efficient, and collaborative team capable of navigating the rapidly changing digital landscape. The company's investment in continuous learning and development ensured sustained growth and innovation.

Question Bank:

2 Marks:

1. What are technical skills, and why are they important in managerial roles?

2. Name three technical skills relevant to digital marketing.

3. What is the significance of financial analysis in the finance sector?

4. Describe one key technical skill necessary for supply chain management

5. Why is cross-functional coordination important for middle managers?

5 Marks:

1. What role do top managers play in strategic decision-making with respect to technical skills?

2. List two strategies for staying updated with industry trend.

3. Discuss the importance of technical skills for front-line managers and provide examples of how these skills are applied in different sectors.

4. Explain the role of technical skills in middle management, focusing on strategic implementation and resource management.

5. How do top managers utilize technical skills to drive innovation and growth within an organization? Provide specific examples.

10 Marks:

1. Describe the various methods through which professionals can continuously develop and maintain technical expertise in a rapidly changing environment.

2. Analyze the impact of effective data analysis on marketing strategies and outcomes. How can marketers enhance their data analysis skills?

3. What are the benefits of cross-training within an organization, and how can it improve collaboration and overall technical proficiency among employees?

4. Explain how leveraging technology and online learning platforms can contribute to the continuous improvement of technical skills. Provide examples of platforms and tools that are beneficial for different functional areas.

Module 5

Global Management Skills

Global management skills are crucial in today's interconnected world, where businesses operate across borders, cultures, and markets. This module explores the significance of global management skills, the challenges and opportunities in global business environments, and strategies for developing cross-cultural competence and managing international teams effectively.

Understanding the Importance of Global Management Skills in Today's Interconnected World

In a globalized economy, organizations must navigate diverse cultural, economic, and political landscapes to compete and thrive. Global management skills refer to the ability to understand, adapt to, and effectively manage the complexities of international business operations. These skills are essential for leaders and managers to make informed decisions, build strategic partnerships, and drive sustainable growth in global markets.

Key Aspects of Global Management Skills:

1. **Cultural Intelligence**: Understanding and appreciating cultural differences in values, communication styles, and business practices. Cultural intelligence enables managers to navigate cultural nuances, build trust across borders, and foster collaboration in diverse teams.
2. **Strategic Thinking**: Developing global strategies that align with organizational goals and market opportunities. Strategic thinking involves analyzing global trends, identifying competitive advantages, and adapting business strategies to diverse cultural contexts.
3. **Cross-Cultural Communication**: Communicating effectively across cultures to convey messages clearly, build relationships, and resolve conflicts. Managers with strong cross-cultural

communication skills bridge linguistic and cultural barriers, enhancing teamwork and organizational effectiveness.
4. **Global Leadership**: Leading diverse teams and organizations with cultural sensitivity, empathy, and inclusivity. Global leaders inspire and motivate international teams, promote diversity and inclusion, and drive innovation in global markets.
5. **Adaptability and Resilience**: Adapting to changing global environments, economic fluctuations, and geopolitical challenges. Managers with adaptability and resilience navigate uncertainty, mitigate risks, and capitalize on emerging opportunities in global markets.
6. **Ethical and Social Responsibility**: Integrating ethical principles and corporate social responsibility (CSR) into global business practices. Responsible global managers prioritize ethical conduct, environmental sustainability, and social impact to enhance brand reputation and stakeholder trust

Challenges and Opportunities in Global Business Environments

Global business environments present both challenges and opportunities for organizations seeking to expand internationally and achieve sustainable growth. Understanding these dynamics is essential for developing effective strategies and mitigating risks in global markets.

Challenges:

1. **Cultural Differences**: Managing cultural diversity and navigating cultural differences in values, norms, and communication styles can lead to misunderstandings, conflicts, and operational challenges.
2. **Geopolitical Risks**: Political instability, trade barriers, regulatory complexities, and geopolitical tensions can impact market entry, operations, and supply chain management in global markets.
3. **Market Saturation and Competition**: Intense competition, market saturation, and price wars pose challenges for organizations entering or expanding in competitive global markets.
4. **Operational Complexities**: Managing dispersed teams, coordinating global supply chains, and ensuring consistent

quality standards across different markets require robust operational strategies and logistical expertise.
5. **Legal and Regulatory Compliance**: Navigating diverse legal systems, compliance requirements, and international regulations poses legal risks and operational challenges for global businesses.

Opportunities:

1. **Market Expansion**: Accessing new markets, untapped consumer segments, and emerging economies offers growth opportunities for expanding market presence and diversifying revenue streams.
2. **Strategic Partnerships**: Forming strategic alliances, joint ventures, and partnerships with local businesses or multinational corporations facilitates market entry, enhances market knowledge, and strengthens competitive positioning.
3. **Innovation and Technology**: Leveraging technological advancements, digital platforms, and innovation hubs to drive product innovation, operational efficiency, and customer engagement in global markets.
4. **Talent Acquisition and Diversity**: Attracting diverse talent pools, leveraging local expertise, and promoting cultural diversity enhance creativity, innovation, and organizational resilience in global teams.
5. **Brand Differentiation**: Building a strong global brand identity, reputation for quality, and customer loyalty through effective marketing strategies and customer-centric initiatives.

Strategies for Developing Cross-Cultural Competence and Managing International Teams: Effective cross-cultural competence and team management are critical for fostering collaboration, maximizing productivity, and achieving organizational goals in diverse global environments. Managers can implement strategies to develop cultural intelligence, build cohesive international teams, and promote inclusive leadership.

Strategies for Developing Cross-Cultural Competence:

1. **Cultural Training and Education**: Provide cultural awareness training, workshops, and language courses to educate employees on cultural norms, values, and communication styles in target markets. Enhance cultural sensitivity and adaptability among team members.
2. **Immersive Experiences**: Facilitate cross-cultural exchanges, international assignments, and immersion programs to expose employees to diverse cultural environments and promote firsthand learning experiences.
3. **Cultural Mentorship and Coaching**: Pair employees with mentors or coaches from different cultural backgrounds to foster cross-cultural understanding, mentorship relationships, and professional development.
4. **Intercultural Communication Skills**: Develop intercultural communication skills, such as active listening, empathy, and cross-cultural negotiation, to facilitate effective communication and relationship-building across cultural boundaries.
5. **Cultural Intelligence Assessments**: Use cultural intelligence assessments and feedback mechanisms to evaluate and enhance employees' cultural competence, adaptability, and effectiveness in global roles.

Strategies for Managing International Teams:

1. **Clear Communication Channels**: Establish clear communication channels, protocols, and language proficiency standards to facilitate effective communication and information sharing among international team members.
2. **Team Diversity and Inclusion**: Promote diversity and inclusion initiatives, celebrate cultural holidays, and create opportunities for cultural exchange to foster a sense of belonging and cohesion within international teams.
3. **Shared Goals and Objectives**: Align team goals, objectives, and performance metrics with organizational priorities to enhance team cohesion, collaboration, and accountability across geographical boundaries.
4. **Virtual Collaboration Tools**: Implement virtual collaboration tools, project management platforms, and video conferencing technology to facilitate real-time collaboration, document sharing, and remote team meetings.

5. **Conflict Resolution Strategies**: Develop conflict resolution strategies, cultural mediation techniques, and cross-cultural sensitivity training to address conflicts, misunderstandings, and cultural differences within international teams.

By understanding the importance of global management skills, addressing challenges and opportunities in global business environments, and implementing strategies for cross-cultural competence and international team management, managers can effectively lead global initiatives, drive organizational success, and foster a culture of innovation and collaboration across borders. These strategies empower organizations to navigate complexities, capitalize on global opportunities, and achieve sustainable growth in today's interconnected world.

Case Study: Global Management Skills at Tech Innovators Inc.

Background:

Tech Innovators Inc., a leading technology company, has grown exponentially over the past decade, establishing its presence in various international markets. Headquartered in Silicon Valley, the company specializes in cutting-edge software solutions and has regional offices in Europe, Asia, and South America. Recognizing the importance of a global footprint, the company embarked on an ambitious expansion strategy to leverage new market opportunities and diversify its revenue streams.

Issues Faced:

As Tech Innovators Inc. expanded its operations globally, the company encountered several challenges:

1. **Cultural Differences**: The management team struggled to navigate the diverse cultural landscapes across their international offices. Differences in work ethics, communication styles, and business practices led to misunderstandings and reduced team cohesion.

2. **Cross-Cultural Communication**: Ineffective communication across different cultures created barriers in project execution and team collaboration. Language differences and varying communication norms caused delays and frustration among team members.
3. **Geopolitical Risks**: Political instability and regulatory complexities in certain regions posed significant risks to the company's operations. Navigating these risks required a deep understanding of local political and legal environments.
4. **Talent Management**: Attracting and retaining talent in different regions proved challenging. The company faced difficulties in understanding local labor markets and developing competitive compensation and benefit packages.
5. **Operational Complexities**: Coordinating efforts across geographically dispersed teams and maintaining consistent quality standards were operational hurdles. Variations in time zones further complicated project management and decision-making processes.

Strategies to Improve

To address these challenges and improve its global management capabilities, Tech Innovators Inc. implemented several strategies:

1. **Cultural Training and Education**: The company introduced comprehensive cultural awareness training programs for employees at all levels. These programs included workshops, seminars, and language courses to enhance understanding of cultural norms, values, and communication styles in different markets. This initiative helped employees develop cultural intelligence and adapt their behavior to diverse cultural contexts.
2. **Cross-Cultural Mentorship**: Tech Innovators Inc. established a cross-cultural mentorship program, pairing employees from different cultural backgrounds. This initiative fostered mutual learning, cultural exchange, and professional development. Mentors provided guidance on navigating cultural nuances, building trust, and enhancing cross-cultural collaboration.

3. **Clear Communication Channels**: The company standardized communication protocols and language proficiency standards across all international offices. It also implemented advanced virtual collaboration tools, such as project management platforms and video conferencing technology, to facilitate real-time communication and document sharing. These tools bridged linguistic and cultural barriers, ensuring effective communication and teamwork.
4. **Geopolitical Risk Management**: To mitigate geopolitical risks, Tech Innovators Inc. established a dedicated risk management team. This team conducted thorough analyses of political and regulatory environments in different regions and developed risk mitigation strategies. The company also formed strategic alliances with local businesses to navigate complex regulatory landscapes and enhance market entry.
5. **Talent Acquisition and Retention**: Tech Innovators Inc. revamped its talent management strategies to attract and retain diverse talent pools. The company conducted market research to understand local labor markets and developed competitive compensation packages tailored to regional preferences. It also promoted diversity and inclusion initiatives to create a supportive and inclusive work environment, celebrating cultural holidays and encouraging cultural exchange.
6. **Global Leadership Development**: The company invested in leadership development programs focused on global leadership skills. These programs emphasized cultural sensitivity, empathy, and inclusivity. Leaders were trained to inspire and motivate international teams, fostering a culture of innovation and collaboration

Outcomes

By implementing these strategies, Tech Innovators Inc. significantly improved its global management capabilities. The company's cultural intelligence and cross-cultural communication skills enhanced team cohesion and operational efficiency. Effective risk management strategies allowed the company to navigate geopolitical challenges and sustain operations in volatile regions. Improved talent management and leadership development initiatives attracted and retained top talent, driving innovation and growth.

Tech Innovators Inc. successfully capitalized on global opportunities, achieving sustainable growth and strengthening its position as a leading player in the international technology market. The company's commitment to cultural competence and global leadership set a benchmark for effective global management in today's interconnected world.

Question Bank

5 Marks:

1. **What is cultural intelligence, and why is it crucial for global managers?**

1. **How does strategic thinking benefit global management?**
2. **What are the main barriers to effective cross-cultural communication?**
3. **Why is adaptability important for managers in global markets?**
4. **How do ethical practices and CSR contribute to global business success?**
5. **What are some common challenges organizations face in global business environments?**
6. **What role do virtual collaboration tools play in managing international teams?**

10 Marks:

1. **Explain the concept of cultural intelligence and discuss how it can be developed and applied in a global management context. Provide specific examples of situations where cultural intelligence has significantly impacted business outcomes.**
2. **Discuss the role of strategic thinking in global management. How can managers align global strategies with organizational goals while considering diverse cultural contexts? Include examples of successful global strategies.**
3. **Evaluate the challenges of cross-cultural communication in international business. What techniques and strategies can managers use to overcome these challenges and enhance communication effectiveness across cultures?**

4. Analyze the importance of adaptability and resilience in global management. How can managers develop these skills to navigate economic fluctuations, geopolitical challenges, and other uncertainties in global markets?

5. Discuss the ethical considerations and corporate social responsibility (CSR) initiatives that global managers must integrate into their business practices. How do these initiatives impact brand reputation and stakeholder trust? Provide case studies of successful CSR programs.

6. Identify and explain the key challenges faced by organizations when entering and operating in new global markets. How can managers mitigate these challenges and leverage opportunities for sustainable growth?

7. Explore the strategies for developing cross-cultural competence within an organization. How can cultural training, immersive experiences, and mentorship programs enhance employees' cultural intelligence and effectiveness in global roles?

Module 6

Leadership and Influence

1.Characteristics of Effective Leadership in Managerial Roles

Vision and Strategic Thinking

Effective leaders are visionary. They not only see the big picture but also articulate a clear, compelling vision that inspires their team. This vision acts as a roadmap, guiding the organization towards long-term goals. Strategic thinking complements vision by enabling leaders to develop actionable plans to achieve these goals. It involves analyzing the internal and external environment, identifying opportunities and threats, and formulating strategies that leverage strengths and mitigate weaknesses.

For instance, a leader at a tech company might foresee the potential of artificial intelligence and steer the company towards AI-driven innovations. This visionary approach not only sets a direction but also motivates the team by aligning their efforts with a meaningful purpose.

Communication Skills

Effective communication is a cornerstone of leadership. Leaders must convey their vision, goals, and expectations clearly and transparently. This builds trust and ensures everyone is aligned. Effective leaders are also good listeners; they value input from their team, fostering an inclusive environment where everyone feels heard and valued.

For example, a manager who regularly holds team meetings to discuss project progress, address concerns, and seek feedback exemplifies good communication. This practice ensures that team members are on the same page and feel involved in decision-making processes.

Emotional Intelligence

Emotional intelligence (EI) is the ability to understand and manage one's own emotions and those of others. Leaders with high EI are self-aware, recognizing their strengths and weaknesses. They exhibit empathy, understanding the emotions and perspectives of their team members. This empathy helps in building strong relationships, resolving conflicts, and fostering a supportive work environment.

Consider a scenario where a team is under high stress due to a tight deadline. An emotionally intelligent leader would recognize the signs of stress, provide support, and perhaps adjust workloads or deadlines to maintain morale and productivity.

Integrity and Ethical Behaviour

Trustworthiness is crucial for effective leadership. Leaders with integrity adhere to ethical principles and act consistently with their values. They are accountable, taking responsibility for their actions and decisions. This builds trust and respect among team members, who are more likely to follow a leader they believe is honest and fair.

For instance, a leader who admits to a mistake and takes steps to rectify it, rather than deflecting blame, demonstrates integrity. This behaviour sets a positive example and fosters a culture of accountability within the team.

Adaptability and Resilience

In today's dynamic business environment, adaptability is essential. Effective leaders are flexible, open to new ideas, and willing to change course when necessary. Resilience, the ability to recover from setbacks, is equally important. Resilient leaders maintain a positive outlook and inspire confidence in their team, even during challenging times.

For example, during the COVID-19 pandemic, many leaders had to pivot quickly to remote work models. Those who adapted swiftly and supported their teams through the transition demonstrated effective leadership.

Decision-Making Skills

Leaders are often required to make tough decisions. Effective decision-making involves analytical thinking and decisiveness. Leaders must gather relevant information, consider various options, and weigh the pros and cons before deciding. They should also be able to make timely decisions to prevent delays and keep the organization moving forward.

A leader deciding on whether to invest in a new project might analyse market trends, assess risks, and consult with key stakeholders before making a final call. This balanced approach ensures well-informed decisions that align with organizational goals.

Motivation and Inspiration

Inspirational leaders motivate their teams by setting high standards, providing encouragement, and recognizing achievements. They create an environment where team members are enthusiastic about their work and committed to achieving organizational goals. Empowering leadership, which involves giving team members autonomy and resources, further enhances motivation.

For instance, a leader who regularly acknowledges individual and team accomplishments fosters a sense of pride and motivation. Empowering employees by delegating responsibilities and trusting them to make decisions also boosts their confidence and engagement.

Relationship Building

Building strong relationships is key to effective leadership. Leaders should foster collaboration and teamwork, creating an environment where individuals feel connected and valued. This involves not only working well with team members but also building networks within and outside the organization.

A leader who encourages collaboration by promoting team-building activities, cross-functional projects, and open communication channels enhances the overall cohesion and effectiveness of the team.

2.Different Leadership Styles and Their Impact on Team Performance

Autocratic Leadership

Autocratic leaders make decisions unilaterally, without consulting their team. This style can be effective in situations requiring quick decision-making or when dealing with inexperienced team members. However, it can lead to low morale and high turnover if overused, as team members may feel undervalued and disengaged.

For example, in a crisis where immediate action is needed, an autocratic leader might quickly allocate tasks to ensure swift response. However, in the long term, this style can stifle creativity and reduce team motivation.

Democratic Leadership

Democratic leaders involve their team in decision-making processes. They value input from team members and encourage participation. This style fosters a sense of ownership and collaboration, leading to higher job satisfaction and productivity. However, it can be time-consuming and may not be suitable for all situations, especially those requiring swift action.

A democratic leader might hold regular team meetings to gather ideas and feedback on a new project. This inclusive approach ensures that team members feel valued and are more committed to the project's success.

Transformational Leadership

Transformational leaders inspire and motivate their team by creating a vision for the future and encouraging innovation. They focus on personal and professional development, helping team members achieve their potential. This style can lead to high levels of motivation, engagement, and performance. However, it requires strong communication and emotional intelligence skills.

For instance, a transformational leader in a tech company might encourage employees to pursue new skills and certifications, fostering a culture of continuous learning and innovation.

Transactional Leadership

Transactional leaders focus on routine, supervision, and performance-based rewards and penalties. This style is effective in achieving short-term goals and maintaining order. However, it may not foster long-term motivation or innovation, as it emphasizes compliance over creativity.

A transactional leader might set clear performance targets and provide bonuses for achieving them. While this can drive immediate results, it might not encourage employees to go beyond their specified duties or innovate.

Laissez-Faire Leadership

Laissez-faire leaders provide minimal direction and allow their team to make decisions. This style can be effective when leading highly skilled and self-motivated teams. However, it can lead to a lack of direction and accountability if team members are not sufficiently experienced or disciplined.

For example, a leader in a research and development team might adopt a laissez-faire approach, giving researchers the freedom to explore new ideas and solutions. This can lead to innovation but requires a high level of self-discipline among team members.

Situational Leadership

Situational leaders adapt their style based on the needs of their team and the specific circumstances. They may switch between autocratic, democratic, transformational, and other styles as needed. This flexibility can lead to effective leadership, as it considers the context and the team's maturity and competence.

A situational leader might take a more autocratic approach during a crisis but switch to a democratic style during regular operations to foster collaboration and innovation.

3.Techniques for Inspiring and Motivating Teams to Achieve Goals

Setting Clear Goals and Expectations

Clear, achievable goals provide direction and purpose. Effective leaders set SMART (Specific, Measurable, Achievable, Relevant, Time-bound) goals that align with the organization's vision. They communicate these goals clearly and ensure that team members understand their roles and responsibilities.

For instance, a leader might set a goal for the sales team to increase revenue by 10% over the next quarter. By breaking this down into specific tasks and milestones, the team can focus their efforts and track progress.

Providing Regular Feedback and Recognition

Feedback is crucial for growth and improvement. Leaders should provide constructive feedback regularly, highlighting both strengths and areas for development. Recognition and rewards for achievements also boost motivation and morale.

A leader might implement a weekly feedback session where team members discuss their progress and challenges. Recognizing accomplishments during these sessions reinforces positive behaviour and motivates the team to strive for excellence.

Creating a Positive Work Environment

A positive work environment fosters motivation and productivity. Leaders should promote a culture of respect, inclusivity, and collaboration. Providing a supportive and flexible work environment, encouraging work-life balance, and addressing any issues promptly contribute to a positive atmosphere.

For example, a leader might establish an open-door policy, encouraging team members to share their concerns and ideas freely. This openness builds trust and creates a more engaged and motivated workforce.

Empowering Team Members

Empowerment involves giving team members the autonomy to make decisions and take ownership of their work. Leaders should delegate tasks, provide the necessary resources and support, and trust their team to deliver results.

A leader might empower a team member by assigning them to lead a project. This responsibility not only boosts their confidence but also encourages them to innovate and take initiative.

Encouraging Personal and Professional Development

Investing in the personal and professional development of team members shows that leaders value their growth. Providing opportunities for training, mentorship, and career advancement motivates employees to improve their skills and performance.

For instance, a leader might support an employee's pursuit of further education or certification relevant to their role. This investment in development fosters loyalty and encourages continuous improvement.

Fostering a Sense of Purpose and Meaning

Connecting team members' work to the larger organizational mission and values helps them see the significance of their contributions. Leaders should regularly communicate how individual and team efforts impact the organization's success.

A leader might share stories of how the team's work has positively impacted customers or contributed to the community. This connection to a greater purpose can be a powerful motivator.

Building Strong Relationships and Team Cohesion

Strong relationships and a cohesive team enhance collaboration and performance. Leaders should facilitate team-building activities, promote open communication, and create opportunities for team members to bond.

For example, organizing team retreats or social events can strengthen relationships and build a sense of camaraderie. When team members trust and support each other, they are more motivated to work towards common goals.

Leading by Example

Leaders who model the behaviours and attitudes they expect from their team inspire trust and respect. Leading by example in areas such as work ethic, integrity, and professionalism sets a standard for the team to follow.

A leader who consistently demonstrates commitment, punctuality, and a positive attitude creates a culture of excellence that motivates the entire team to emulate these qualities.

Providing the Right Tools and Resources

Ensuring that team members have the tools, resources, and support they need to succeed is critical. Leaders should assess the needs of their team and remove any barriers to performance.

For instance, investing in up-to-date technology, providing access to relevant information, and ensuring a comfortable work environment enable team members to perform at their best.

Encouraging Innovation and Creativity

Innovation and creativity drive progress and motivation. Leaders should create an environment where new ideas are welcomed, and experimentation is encouraged. Supporting risk-taking and learning from failures fosters a culture of innovation.

A leader might set up an innovation lab or regular brainstorming sessions where team members can freely share and develop new ideas. This encouragement of creativity keeps the team engaged and motivated to contribute to the organization's success.

By embodying these characteristics, understanding the impact of different leadership styles, and employing techniques to inspire and motivate teams, leaders can effectively guide their organizations toward achieving their goals and fostering a positive, productive work environment.

Case Study: Leadership Transformation at InnovateTech

Background

InnovateTech, a mid-sized technology company, specializes in developing cutting-edge software solutions. Despite having a talented team and a strong product lineup, the company was struggling with declining employee morale, high turnover rates, and stagnant innovation. The CEO, Sarah Collins, realized that the root cause of these issues lay in the company's leadership approach, which was predominantly autocratic and transactional.

Problem Faced

1. **Lack of Vision and Strategic Direction**: The company lacked a clear vision for the future, leaving employees uncertain about the long-term goals.
2. **Poor Communication**: There was a significant communication gap between management and employees, leading to misunderstandings and misalignment.
3. **Low Employee Morale**: The autocratic leadership style stifled creativity and engagement, resulting in low morale and high turnover.
4. **Resistance to Change**: The company was slow to adapt to market changes and new technologies, hindering innovation.

Strategic Solutions

1. Vision and Strategic Thinking Sarah took the first step by articulating a clear, compelling vision for InnovateTech, focused on becoming a leader in AI-driven software solutions. She communicated this vision through all-hands meetings, detailed presentations, and regular updates, ensuring every employee understood and aligned with the company's long-term goals.

2. Enhancing Communication Skills To bridge the communication gap, Sarah implemented a more inclusive and transparent communication strategy. She held weekly team meetings to discuss project progress, address concerns, and gather feedback. Additionally, she introduced an open-door policy, encouraging employees to share their ideas and issues directly with the leadership.

3. Fostering Emotional Intelligence Sarah recognized the importance of emotional intelligence in leadership. She conducted workshops on emotional intelligence and empathy, helping managers develop better self-awareness and understand their team's emotions. This initiative led to improved relationships, better conflict resolution, and a more supportive work environment.

4. Integrity and Ethical Behavior To build trust and foster a culture of accountability, Sarah emphasized the importance of integrity. She led by example, admitting to her mistakes and taking responsibility for them. This behavior inspired the management team to follow suit, creating a culture of honesty and ethical behavior.

5. Promoting Adaptability and Resilience Sarah encouraged a culture of adaptability and resilience. She supported continuous learning and development, providing resources for employees to acquire new skills and adapt to changing market demands. During the COVID-19 pandemic, she swiftly transitioned the company to a remote work model, ensuring that employees had the necessary tools and support to maintain productivity.

6. Decision-Making Skills Sarah improved the decision-making process by involving key stakeholders in major decisions. She gathered relevant information, weighed pros and cons, and made timely decisions that aligned with the company's strategic goals. This approach not only ensured well-informed decisions but also fostered a sense of ownership among employees.

7. Motivation and Inspiration Sarah motivated her team by setting high standards and recognizing achievements. She implemented a reward system that acknowledged individual and team accomplishments, fostering a sense of pride and motivation. Empowering employees by delegating responsibilities and trusting them to make decisions further boosted their confidence and engagement.

8. Relationship Building To enhance collaboration and teamwork, Sarah organized team-building activities and promoted cross-functional projects. These initiatives helped build strong relationships within the team and improved overall cohesion and effectiveness.

Outcome:

Within a year, InnovateTech experienced a significant turnaround. Employee morale improved, turnover rates decreased, and innovation flourished. The company successfully launched several AI-driven software solutions, positioning itself as a leader in the industry. By embodying effective leadership characteristics and employing strategic solutions, Sarah transformed InnovateTech into a thriving, innovative, and motivated organization.

Question Bank:

2 Marks:

1.What are the key elements of a compelling vision in leadership?

2.Why is effective communication considered a cornerstone of leadership?

3. How does emotional intelligence contribute to effective leadership?

4.What role does integrity play in building team trust?

5.How can recognizing team achievements boost motivation?

5 Marks:

1. Discuss the importance of clear communication in project management. Provide examples of how poor communication can impact project outcomes.

2.Explain the steps involved in writing a research report. How does a well-written research report contribute to knowledge dissemination and decision-making?

3.Compare and contrast different brainstorming techniques for project development. How can these techniques be applied to improve project communication and innovation?

4.Analyze the challenges of conveying negative messages in business communication. How can empathy and sensitivity be integrated into communication strategies to address negative messages effectively?

5.Evaluate the role of standardized reporting in project management. How does standardized reporting contribute to project transparency, accountability, and decision-making?

10 Marks:

1. How can organizations overcome communication challenges to improve project performance and success rates?

2. How can project managers foster stakeholder participation and collaboration through strategic communication initiatives?

3. How do research report writing guidelines contribute to the credibility, validity, and relevance of research findings in academic and professional contexts?

4. How can leaders effectively develop and communicate a vision that aligns with organizational goals and inspires their team?

5. Discuss the importance of communication skills in leadership. How can leaders ensure clear and transparent communication within their teams?

6.Why is integrity crucial for leadership? Discuss the impact of ethical behavior on team trust and organizational culture.

7.Discuss techniques leaders can use to inspire and motivate their teams. How does recognizing achievements contribute to team motivation?

8.Compare and contrast autocratic and democratic leadership styles. How do these styles impact team performance and morale?

Module 7

Problem-Solving and Decision-Making

1. Frameworks for Systematic Problem-Solving and Decision-Making

Systematic problem-solving and decision-making are essential skills for managers to effectively navigate challenges and achieve organizational goals. These processes involve structured approaches and frameworks that help clarify issues, analyse information, evaluate options, and implement effective solutions.

Problem-Solving Frameworks

1. **Define the Problem**: The first step in problem-solving is to clearly define the problem or challenge. This involves identifying the symptoms and root causes of the issue. Effective problem definition sets the stage for finding appropriate solutions.
2. **Gather Information**: Once the problem is defined, gather relevant information and data. This may involve conducting research, analyzing trends, consulting stakeholders, and reviewing past experiences. Information gathering ensures a comprehensive understanding of the issue and informs decision-making.
3. **Brainstorm Solutions**: Encourage creative thinking and generate potential solutions to address the problem. Brainstorming sessions involve generating ideas without criticism, allowing for a wide range of possibilities to be considered. This step promotes innovation and identifies diverse approaches to solving the problem.
4. **Evaluate Options**: Evaluate each potential solution based on criteria such as feasibility, cost-effectiveness, alignment with organizational goals, and potential impact. Consider the advantages and disadvantages of each option to determine which one is most suitable.
5. **Make a Decision**: Select the best solution based on the evaluation of options. Consider input from stakeholders, data analysis, and strategic priorities when making decisions. Ensure

decisions are aligned with the organization's mission, values, and long-term objectives.

6. **Implement the Solution**: Develop an action plan and implement the chosen solution. Assign responsibilities, allocate resources, and set clear timelines for implementation. Monitor progress closely to ensure the solution is effectively implemented and achieves the desired outcomes.

Decision-Making Frameworks

1. **Rational Decision-Making**: This approach involves systematically analyzing options, predicting outcomes based on available information, and selecting the most rational choice. Rational decision-making relies on logic, reason, and objective analysis to minimize biases and make informed decisions.

2. **Intuitive Decision-Making**: Intuition plays a role in decision-making when there is insufficient information or time constraints. Intuitive decisions are based on gut feelings, past experiences, and subconscious processing of information. While less structured than rational decision-making, intuition can lead to quick, effective decisions in certain situations.

3. **Decision Trees**: Decision trees are graphical representations of decisions and their potential consequences. They help visualize the possible outcomes of different choices and identify the optimal path forward. Decision trees are particularly useful for complex decisions involving multiple variables and uncertain outcomes.

4. **Cost-Benefit Analysis**: This framework involves weighing the costs and benefits associated with each decision option. Calculate the financial and non-financial costs of implementation against the expected benefits to determine whether the decision is economically viable and beneficial to the organization.

5. **SWOT Analysis**: SWOT (Strengths, Weaknesses, Opportunities, Threats) analysis is a strategic planning tool used to evaluate the internal strengths and weaknesses of an organization and external opportunities and threats in the market. It helps identify strategic options and make informed decisions based on the organization's competitive position.

2. How to Gather Relevant Information, Analyze Options, and Implement Solutions

Effective problem-solving and decision-making require systematic approaches to gather relevant information, analyze options, and implement solutions that address organizational challenges and opportunities.

Gathering Relevant Information

1. **Define Information Needs**: Clearly define the information needed to understand the problem or decision at hand. Identify key questions and objectives to guide the information gathering process.
2. **Sources of Information**: Utilize a variety of sources to gather relevant information, including internal data, market research, customer feedback, industry reports, and expert opinions. Consider the credibility, reliability, and relevance of each information source.
3. **Data Collection Methods**: Collect data through methods such as surveys, interviews, focus groups, observation, and data analysis. Use quantitative and qualitative data collection techniques to gain a comprehensive understanding of the problem or decision context.
4. **Data Analysis**: Analyze collected data to identify patterns, trends, correlations, and insights relevant to the problem or decision. Use statistical analysis, data visualization tools, and qualitative analysis techniques to derive meaningful conclusions.

Analyzing Options

1. **Generate Alternative Solutions**: Brainstorm and generate multiple potential solutions to address the identified problem or decision. Consider diverse perspectives and creative ideas to expand the range of options available.
2. **Evaluate Criteria and Prioritize**: Establish criteria for evaluating options, such as feasibility, cost-effectiveness, alignment with

organizational goals, and potential risks. Prioritize options based on these criteria to identify the most promising solutions.
3. **Decision-Making Techniques**: Apply decision-making frameworks such as rational decision-making, intuitive decision-making, decision trees, and cost-benefit analysis to evaluate and compare options objectively. Consider the potential outcomes, risks, and implications of each option.
4. **Consult Stakeholders**: Seek input and feedback from relevant stakeholders, including team members, subject matter experts, and key decision-makers. Engage stakeholders in the decision-making process to gain diverse perspectives and ensure buy-in for the chosen solution.

Implementing Solutions

1. **Develop an Action Plan**: Create a detailed action plan outlining the steps, resources, responsibilities, and timelines required to implement the chosen solution. Establish clear objectives and milestones to monitor progress and measure success.
2. **Allocate Resources**: Allocate necessary resources, such as budget, personnel, technology, and materials, to support the implementation of the solution. Ensure resources are sufficient and aligned with the requirements of the action plan.
3. **Communication and Stakeholder Engagement**: Communicate the chosen solution and implementation plan to relevant stakeholders, ensuring transparency and clarity. Engage stakeholders throughout the implementation process to address concerns, obtain support, and foster collaboration.
4. **Monitor and Evaluate Progress**: Monitor the implementation progress closely to identify any challenges or deviations from the action plan. Evaluate the effectiveness of the solution based on predefined metrics and key performance indicators (KPIs).
5. **Adjust and Refine**: Be prepared to adjust the implementation approach based on real-time feedback and emerging insights. Adapt the action plan as needed to optimize outcomes and overcome obstacles encountered during implementation.

3.Case Studies or Examples Illustrating Effective Problem-Solving Techniques

Case Study 1: Toyota's Lean Manufacturing

Toyota implemented the Lean Manufacturing philosophy to address inefficiencies and improve production processes. By identifying and eliminating waste in production, such as overproduction, defects, and unnecessary inventory, Toyota optimized resource utilization and enhanced productivity. This systematic approach to problem-solving allowed Toyota to maintain high product quality while reducing costs and lead times, setting a benchmark for efficiency in the automotive industry.

Case Study 2: NASA's Decision-Making in Apollo 13 Mission

During the Apollo 13 mission, NASA faced a critical situation when an oxygen tank exploded, jeopardizing the lives of astronauts. NASA engineers and mission control utilized systematic problem-solving and decision-making processes to devise solutions under extreme pressure. They conducted thorough root cause analysis, evaluated alternative options for oxygen supply, and implemented innovative engineering solutions, such as using onboard resources creatively. This collaborative effort and systematic approach enabled NASA to safely return the astronauts to Earth, demonstrating the importance of effective decision-making in crisis situations.

Case Study 3: Amazon's Customer-Centric Innovation

Amazon employs a customer-centric approach to problem-solving and decision-making, focusing on meeting customer needs and preferences. Through data-driven analysis of customer behavior, preferences, and feedback, Amazon identifies opportunities for innovation and improvement. For example, Amazon's introduction of Prime membership was based on customer demand for fast, reliable shipping. This customer-centric innovation not only enhances customer satisfaction but also drives business growth and competitive advantage in the e-commerce industry.

These case studies illustrate how organizations apply systematic problem-solving frameworks, gather relevant information, analyze options rigorously, and implement effective solutions to achieve strategic objectives and overcome challenges. By learning from these examples, managers can enhance their problem-solving and decision-making skills, fostering innovation, efficiency, and organizational success.

Question Bank:

2 Marks:

1. What is the first step in systematic problem-solving??

2. Why is gathering relevant information important in problem-solving?

3. What is the purpose of brainstorming in the problem-solving process?

4. Name one criterion used to evaluate potential solutions.

5. Describe intuitive decision-making in one sentence.

5 Marks:

1. Explain the steps involved in the rational decision-making framew

2. Discuss the role of stakeholder consultation in the decision-making process.

3. How does Toyota's Lean Manufacturing approach illustrate effective problem-solving?

4. Describe the process of developing an action plan for implementing a solution.

   Analyze the benefits and drawbacks of using cost-benefit analysis in decision-making

10 Marks:

1. How did NASA's approach to problem-solving during the Apollo 13 mission ensure the safety of the astronauts?

2. What are the key components of Amazon's customer-centric
    approach to innovation, and how does it drive business growth?

71

Module 8

Time and Stress Management

Time and stress management are critical skills for managers to maintain productivity, achieve goals, and sustain well-being in demanding work environments. This module explores strategies for prioritizing tasks and managing time effectively, techniques for reducing stress and maintaining work-life balance, and tools and resources for enhancing personal productivity and resilience.

Strategies for Prioritizing Tasks and Managing Time Effectively

Effective time management is essential for managers to optimize productivity, focus on strategic priorities, and achieve organizational goals efficiently. Implementing strategies for task prioritization and time management empowers managers to make informed decisions, allocate resources effectively, and enhance overall work efficiency.

Key Strategies for Prioritizing Tasks:

1. **ABC Method**: Prioritize tasks based on urgency and importance. Classify tasks as A (urgent and important), B (important but not urgent), and C (less important or can be deferred). Focus on completing high-priority tasks first to meet deadlines and achieve immediate goals.
2. **Eisenhower Matrix**: Use the Eisenhower Matrix to categorize tasks into four quadrants based on urgency and importance:
   - **Quadrant 1 (Urgent and Important)**: Address tasks that require immediate attention and contribute to critical goals.
   - **Quadrant 2 (Important but Not Urgent)**: Allocate time for strategic planning, professional development, and long-term projects.
   - **Quadrant 3 (Urgent but Not Important)**: Delegate or minimize tasks that are urgent but do not align with strategic objectives.
   - **Quadrant 4 (Not Urgent and Not Important)**: Limit time spent on low-priority tasks and avoid distractions.

3. **Time Blocking**: Allocate dedicated time blocks for specific tasks, activities, or projects. Schedule uninterrupted periods for focused work, meetings, email management, and breaks. Time blocking enhances productivity, minimizes multitasking, and improves time management skills.
4. **Priority Setting**: Set SMART (Specific, Measurable, Achievable, Relevant, Time-bound) goals to guide task prioritization and time allocation. Define clear objectives, establish deadlines, and prioritize tasks based on their impact on organizational objectives and project milestones.
5. **Batch Processing**: Group similar tasks together to streamline workflow and minimize context switching. Allocate specific time blocks for activities such as responding to emails, conducting meetings, or completing administrative tasks. Batch processing optimizes efficiency and reduces cognitive load throughout the workday.

Strategies for Managing Time Effectively:

1. **Goal Alignment**: Align daily tasks and activities with overarching goals and strategic priorities. Regularly review and adjust goals to ensure alignment with organizational objectives and optimize resource allocation.
2. **Task Delegation**: Delegate tasks to capable team members based on their skills, expertise, and workload capacity. Empower team members to take ownership of tasks, promote accountability, and foster collaboration within the team.
3. **Proactive Planning**: Plan and organize tasks in advance, create to-do lists, and establish daily, weekly, and monthly schedules. Anticipate potential challenges, allocate sufficient time for task completion, and prioritize activities based on their importance and deadlines.
4. **Time Management Tools**: Utilize digital tools and applications, such as task managers (e.g., Todoist, Asana), calendars (e.g., Google Calendar, Outlook), and time trackers (e.g., Toggl, RescueTime), to plan, organize, and monitor tasks effectively. These tools streamline workflow management, enhance productivity, and optimize time utilization.
5. **Continuous Improvement**: Evaluate and optimize time management strategies regularly. Identify inefficiencies, learn

from past experiences, and implement continuous improvement practices to refine time management skills and enhance overall effectiveness.

2. Techniques for Reducing Stress and Maintaining Work-Life Balance

Stress management and work-life balance are essential for managers to sustain well-being, prevent burnout, and maintain peak performance in demanding professional roles. Implementing effective stress reduction techniques and work-life balance strategies promotes resilience, enhances productivity, and supports long-term career satisfaction.

Effective Techniques for Stress Reduction:

1. **Mindfulness and Meditation**: Practice mindfulness techniques, such as deep breathing exercises, meditation, and mindful awareness, to reduce stress, promote relaxation, and improve mental clarity. Incorporate mindfulness into daily routines to manage stress effectively and enhance emotional well-being.
2. **Physical Exercise**: Engage in regular physical activities, such as yoga, jogging, or strength training, to release endorphins, alleviate tension, and improve overall health. Physical exercise enhances resilience against stress, boosts energy levels, and supports mental and emotional well-being.
3. **Stress Management Courses**: Attend stress management courses, workshops, or seminars to learn effective coping strategies, stress reduction techniques, and relaxation exercises. Develop skills to manage stress proactively, identify triggers, and implement stress-relief practices in daily life.
4. **Time Management**: Implement efficient time management strategies to prioritize tasks, allocate time effectively, and reduce stress from overwhelming workloads. Break down complex projects into manageable steps, establish realistic deadlines, and avoid procrastination to minimize stress levels.
5. **Healthy Lifestyle Choices**: Adopt a balanced diet, stay hydrated, and get sufficient sleep to support physical health and mental resilience. Avoid excessive caffeine or alcohol consumption, which can exacerbate stress and disrupt sleep patterns.

Strategies for Maintaining Work-Life Balance:

1. **Establish Boundaries**: Define clear boundaries between work and personal life to prevent work-related stress and promote well-being. Set specific work hours, designate non-work time for leisure activities, and avoid bringing work-related tasks into personal time.
2. **Schedule Leisure Activities**: Allocate time for hobbies, interests, and social activities to recharge and unwind outside of work commitments. Schedule regular breaks, vacations, and downtime to relax, rejuvenate, and maintain a healthy work-life balance.
3. **Flexible Work Arrangements**: Negotiate flexible work arrangements, such as telecommuting or flexible hours, to accommodate personal needs and promote work-life integration. Balance professional responsibilities with personal obligations and prioritize self-care to enhance overall well-being.
4. **Time for Self-Care**: Dedicate time for self-care practices, such as reading, listening to music, or pursuing creative hobbies. Engage in activities that promote relaxation, reduce stress levels, and foster personal growth outside of work responsibilities.
5. **Support Networks**: Build strong support networks with colleagues, friends, and family members to seek emotional support, share experiences, and maintain social connections. Cultivate relationships that provide encouragement, perspective, and resilience during challenging times.

3.Tools and Resources for Enhancing Personal Productivity and Resilience

Enhancing personal productivity and resilience equips managers with the skills, tools, and resources to optimize performance, navigate challenges, and achieve professional success in dynamic work environments. Leveraging productivity tools, adopting resilience-building strategies, and investing in personal development empower managers to thrive amidst complexity and uncertainty.

Tools for Enhancing Personal Productivity:

1. **Task Management Apps**: Utilize task management applications, such as Todoist, Trello, or Microsoft To Do, to organize tasks, set deadlines, and track progress. These apps streamline workflow management, prioritize tasks, and ensure timely completion of assignments.
2. **Time Tracking Software**: Implement time tracking tools, such as Toggl, RescueTime, or Clockify, to monitor time spent on tasks, analyze productivity patterns, and identify areas for improvement. Time tracking enhances accountability, optimizes time allocation, and increases productivity.
3. **Project Management Platforms**: Use project management platforms, such as Asana, Basecamp, or Jira, to collaborate on projects, allocate resources, and manage project timelines effectively. These platforms facilitate communication, streamline task delegation, and promote team productivity.
4. **Note-Taking Apps**: Employ note-taking applications, such as Evernote, OneNote, or Notion, to capture ideas, organize information, and create actionable plans. Note-taking apps enhance information retention, facilitate knowledge management, and support decision-making processes.
5. **Digital Calendars**: Integrate digital calendars, such as Google Calendar, Outlook, or Apple Calendar, to schedule meetings, set reminders, and manage appointments efficiently. Digital calendars synchronize across devices, streamline schedule management, and optimize time utilization.

Resources for Building Resilience:

1. **Professional Development Programs**: Participate in professional development programs, workshops, or seminars to enhance leadership skills, adaptability, and resilience. Continuous learning fosters personal growth, expands professional capabilities, and prepares managers to navigate challenges effectively.
2. **Stress Management Courses**: Enroll in stress management courses or workshops to learn effective coping strategies, relaxation techniques, and mindfulness practices. Stress management training promotes self-care, mitigates workplace stressors, and enhances resilience against adversity.

3. **Peer Support Networks**: Engage in peer support networks, mentorship programs, or professional associations to connect with industry peers, share experiences, and exchange best practices. Peer support networks provide emotional encouragement, foster collaboration, and promote resilience in challenging work environments.
4. **Wellness Initiatives**: Participate in workplace wellness initiatives, such as wellness programs, fitness classes, or mindfulness sessions, to promote physical health, mental well-being, and work-life balance. Wellness initiatives encourage healthy lifestyle choices, reduce stress levels, and enhance overall resilience.
5. **Resilience-Building Books and Resources**: Read resilience-building books, articles, or blogs that offer insights, strategies, and practical tips for developing resilience in professional and personal life. Learning from resilience experts and thought leaders enhances self-awareness, strengthens coping skills, and inspires continuous growth.

By implementing strategies for prioritizing tasks, managing time effectively, reducing stress, maintaining work-life balance, and leveraging tools for personal productivity and resilience, managers can optimize performance, enhance well-being, and achieve sustainable success in their professional roles. These practices empower managers to navigate challenges proactively, foster resilience amidst uncertainty, and cultivate a positive work environment conducive to growth and achievement.

Case Study: Enhancing Time and Stress Management at XYZ Corporation

Background

XYZ Corporation, a leading technology company, is renowned for its innovative products and rapid growth. However, the company faces challenges in managing the increasing workload, meeting project deadlines, and maintaining employee well-being. The fast-paced environment and high demands have led to increased stress levels and decreased productivity among managers and employees.

Problem Faced

Managers at XYZ Corporation struggle with time management and stress, resulting in:

- Missed deadlines and delayed projects.
- High levels of stress and burnout among managers and employees.
- Decreased overall productivity and efficiency.
- Poor work-life balance and employee dissatisfaction.

Strategic Solution to Improve the Issues

To address these issues, XYZ Corporation implemented a comprehensive strategy focusing on prioritizing tasks, managing time effectively, reducing stress, and maintaining work-life balance.

Strategies for Prioritizing Tasks and Managing Time Effectively

- **ABC Method**: Managers were trained to prioritize tasks based on urgency and importance, classifying them as A (urgent and important), B (important but not urgent), and C (less important or can be deferred). High-priority tasks were focused on first to meet deadlines and achieve immediate goals.
- **Eisenhower Matrix**: Tasks were categorized into four quadrants based on urgency and importance, helping managers focus on critical goals and strategic planning. This allowed delegation or minimization of less critical tasks, improving overall task management.
- **Time Blocking**: Dedicated time blocks were allocated for specific tasks, meetings, and breaks. This minimized multitasking and improved focus and productivity.
- **Priority Setting with SMART Goals**: Managers set SMART (Specific, Measurable, Achievable, Relevant, Time-bound) goals to guide task prioritization and time allocation. Clear objectives

and deadlines were established, aligning tasks with organizational objectives.

- **Batch Processing**: Similar tasks were grouped together to streamline workflow and minimize context switching. This optimized efficiency and reduced cognitive load throughout the workday.

Techniques for Reducing Stress and Maintaining Work-Life Balance

- **Mindfulness and Meditation**: Managers and employees were encouraged to practice mindfulness techniques, such as deep breathing exercises and meditation. Regular mindfulness sessions were integrated into the daily routine to promote relaxation and mental clarity.
- **Physical Exercise**: The company provided on-site fitness facilities and organized group exercise sessions. Regular physical activity was promoted to release endorphins, alleviate tension, and improve overall health.
- **Stress Management Courses**: Stress management courses and workshops were offered to teach effective coping strategies and relaxation exercises. Managers learned to proactively manage stress and implement stress-relief practices.
- **Time Management**: Efficient time management strategies were implemented to prioritize tasks and reduce stress from overwhelming workloads. Managers were trained to break down complex projects into manageable steps and establish realistic deadlines.
- **Healthy Lifestyle Choices**: The company promoted a balanced diet, hydration, and sufficient sleep. Awareness programs were conducted to avoid excessive caffeine or alcohol consumption, which could exacerbate stress and disrupt sleep patterns.

Tools and Resources for Enhancing Personal Productivity and Resilience

- **Task Management Apps**: Applications like Todoist and Trello were introduced to organize tasks, set deadlines, and track progress. These apps streamlined workflow management and ensured timely completion of assignments.

- **Time Tracking Software**: Tools such as Toggl and RescueTime were implemented to monitor time spent on tasks and analyze productivity patterns. This enhanced accountability and optimized time allocation.
- **Project Management Platforms**: Platforms like Asana and Basecamp facilitated collaboration on projects, resource allocation, and project timelines. These platforms improved communication and promoted team productivity.
- **Note-Taking Apps**: Applications like Evernote and OneNote were used to capture ideas, organize information, and create actionable plans. These apps enhanced information retention and supported decision-making processes.
- **Digital Calendars**: Digital calendars such as Google Calendar and Outlook were integrated to schedule meetings, set reminders, and manage appointments efficiently. These calendars synchronized across devices, optimizing time utilization.

Results and Impact

By implementing these strategies, XYZ Corporation experienced significant improvements:

- Increased productivity and efficiency in managing tasks and projects.
- Reduced stress levels and improved well-being among managers and employees.
- Enhanced work-life balance, leading to higher employee satisfaction and retention.
- Timely completion of projects and achievement of organizational goals.

Overall, the comprehensive approach to time and stress management empowered managers at XYZ Corporation to optimize performance, maintain well-being, and achieve sustainable success in their professional roles.

Question Bank:

2 Marks:

1. What is the ABC Method for prioritizing tasks?

2. How does the Eisenhower Matrix help in managing tasks?

3. Define SMART goals and their importance in time management.

4. What is time blocking and how does it enhance productivity?

5. Why is task delegation important for effective time management?

5 Marks:

1. Name two techniques for reducing stress in the workplace.

2. What role do digital calendars play in time management?

3. Explain the key strategies for prioritizing tasks and managing time effectively. How can these strategies help managers achieve organizational goals?

4. Describe the techniques for reducing stress and maintaining work-life balance. How can implementing these techniques improve overall employee well-being and productivity?

5. How can task management apps and time tracking software enhance personal productivity and accountability for managers? Provide examples of popular apps and their features.

10 Marks:

1. Discuss the importance of proactive planning and continuous improvement in time management. How can managers implement these practices to optimize their efficiency?

2. Explain the concept of batch processing. How can grouping similar tasks together reduce cognitive load and improve workflow efficiency?

3. Describe the role of professional development programs and stress management courses in building resilience among managers. How can these resources help managers navigate challenges effectively?

4. Discuss the impact of establishing boundaries and scheduling leisure activities on maintaining work-life balance. How can flexible work arrangements contribute to this balance and overall well-being?

Communication and Presentation Skills

Effective communication and presentation skills are essential for managers to convey ideas, inspire action, and build relationships within and outside the organization. This module explores the importance of clear and effective communication in managerial roles, tips for improving written and verbal communication skills, and guidelines for delivering impactful presentations to diverse audiences.

1.Importance of Clear and Effective Communication in Managerial Roles

Clear and effective communication is the cornerstone of successful managerial roles, influencing organizational culture, productivity, and stakeholder relationships. Managers must communicate strategic vision, goals, expectations, and feedback clearly and confidently to inspire trust, alignment, and collaboration among team members and stakeholders.

Key Aspects of Clear and Effective Communication:

1. **Clarity and Precision**: Articulate messages clearly, using precise language and avoiding jargon or ambiguous terms. Clear communication ensures that information is easily understood and minimizes the risk of misinterpretation or confusion.
2. **Active Listening**: Practice active listening to understand others' perspectives, demonstrate empathy, and foster open dialogue. Effective managers listen attentively, ask clarifying questions, and acknowledge feedback to build rapport and strengthen relationships.
3. **Feedback and Transparency**: Provide constructive feedback, performance evaluations, and updates transparently to keep team members informed and engaged. Transparent communication promotes trust, accountability, and a culture of continuous improvement within the organization.
4. **Conflict Resolution**: Navigate conflicts and challenges through open communication, constructive dialogue, and conflict

resolution techniques. Effective managers facilitate productive discussions, address concerns promptly, and seek mutually beneficial solutions to resolve conflicts.

5. **Influence and Persuasion**: Use persuasive communication techniques, storytelling, and evidence-based arguments to influence stakeholders, gain buy-in for initiatives, and drive organizational change. Effective communicators tailor messages to resonate with diverse audiences and inspire action.

6. **Cross-Cultural Communication**: Adapt communication styles and strategies to accommodate cultural differences, language barriers, and diverse perspectives in global or multicultural settings. Cultural competence enhances communication effectiveness and fosters inclusivity within international teams.

2.Tips for Improving Written and Verbal Communication Skills

Enhancing written and verbal communication skills empowers managers to convey ideas clearly, engage audiences effectively, and build credibility as communicators. Adopting best practices and refining communication techniques contributes to professional growth and effective leadership in managerial roles.

Tips for Improving Written Communication:

1. **Clarity and Conciseness**: Structure written messages logically, using clear headings, paragraphs, and bullet points to enhance readability and comprehension. Avoid ambiguous language or complex sentences that may confuse readers.

2. **Grammar and Mechanics**: Pay attention to grammar, punctuation, and spelling to maintain professionalism and credibility in written communication. Proofread documents carefully, use spell-check tools, and seek feedback to refine writing skills.

3. **Audience Understanding**: Tailor written communication to the intended audience's knowledge level, interests, and preferences. Adapt language, tone, and style to resonate with readers and convey information effectively.

4. **Professional Email Etiquette**: Follow professional email etiquette guidelines, including clear subject lines, concise

messages, polite language, and timely responses. Use formal language when appropriate and ensure messages are professional and respectful.

5. **Document Formatting**: Format documents consistently, using headers, subheadings, fonts, and colours to organize information and enhance visual appeal. Use templates or style guides to maintain consistency in document design and presentation.

Tips for Improving Verbal Communication:

1. **Clarity and Enunciation**: Articulate words clearly, speak at a moderate pace, and use proper pronunciation to enhance verbal clarity and comprehension. Avoid mumbling, speaking too quickly, or using filler words (e.g., um, ah).
2. **Active Listening**: Practice active listening skills during conversations, meetings, and presentations to understand speakers' messages fully and respond appropriately. Engage with speakers through nodding, eye contact, and verbal affirmations to demonstrate attentiveness.
3. **Nonverbal Communication**: Pay attention to nonverbal cues, such as body language, facial expressions, and gestures, to convey confidence, openness, and sincerity in verbal communication. Maintain eye contact, use gestures purposefully, and adopt a confident posture to enhance message delivery.
4. **Vocabulary and Language**: Expand vocabulary, use precise language, and vary sentence structure to express ideas effectively and engage listeners. Choose words that convey meaning accurately and avoid jargon or technical terms that may confuse non-specialist audiences.
5. **Empathy and Emotional Intelligence**: Demonstrate empathy, emotional intelligence, and sensitivity to others' emotions during conversations and interactions. Acknowledge perspectives, validate feelings, and respond with empathy to build rapport and trust.

3. Guidelines for Delivering Impactful Presentations to Different Audiences

Delivering impactful presentations requires preparation, confidence, and effective communication skills to engage and persuade diverse audiences. Guidelines for planning, structuring, and delivering presentations enable managers to convey key messages persuasively, facilitate meaningful discussions, and achieve presentation objectives successfully.

Guidelines for Planning and Structuring Presentations:

1. **Define Objectives**: Clarify presentation objectives, key messages, and desired outcomes to guide content development and audience engagement. Align presentation content with audience expectations and organizational goals to achieve desired impact.
2. **Audience Analysis**: Conduct audience analysis to understand demographics, knowledge levels, interests, and preferences. Adapt presentation content, language, and delivery style to resonate with the audience and address their needs effectively.
3. **Content Organization**: Structure presentation content logically, using an introduction, main body, and conclusion to provide context, deliver key points, and summarize key takeaways. Use headings, subheadings, and visuals to organize information coherently and enhance comprehension.
4. **Visual Aids and Media**: Incorporate visual aids, such as slides, charts, graphs, and multimedia, to support key messages, illustrate data, and enhance audience engagement. Use visuals sparingly, ensure readability, and maintain consistency in design and formatting.
5. **Engaging Opening**: Begin presentations with a compelling opening, such as a story, quote, or intriguing fact, to capture audience attention and create interest in the topic. Establish rapport, build credibility, and set the stage for effective communication.

Guidelines for Delivery and Engagement:

1. **Confidence and Poise**: Project confidence, enthusiasm, and poise during presentation delivery to inspire audience confidence and maintain engagement. Practice relaxation

techniques, control nervousness, and maintain a positive demeanor throughout the presentation.

2. **Voice Modulation**: Use voice modulation, intonation, and pacing to emphasize key points, convey enthusiasm, and maintain audience interest. Vary vocal delivery to enhance message clarity, express emotions effectively, and captivate listeners.

3. **Interactive Techniques**: Foster audience interaction through questions, polls, discussions, and interactive activities to encourage participation, gather feedback, and promote learning. Engage audience members actively in the presentation process to enhance retention and understanding.

4. **Effective Body Language**: Use positive body language, such as gestures, facial expressions, and posture, to convey confidence, openness, and enthusiasm during presentations. Maintain eye contact, face the audience, and use movement purposefully to enhance message delivery and audience connection.

5. **Q&A and Feedback Handling**: Facilitate Q&A sessions, address audience questions confidently, and provide clear, concise responses to inquiries. Acknowledge diverse viewpoints, validate feedback, and use questions as opportunities to reinforce key messages and clarify information.

By prioritizing clear and effective communication, refining written and verbal communication skills, and mastering the art of delivering impactful presentations, managers can enhance their influence, build credibility, and foster positive relationships with stakeholders. These skills empower managers to lead effectively, inspire teams, and achieve organizational objectives through effective communication and compelling presentations.

Question Bank:

2 Marks:

1. What is the primary importance of clear and effective communication in managerial roles?

2. Name two key aspects of clear communication mentioned in the module.

3. What are the benefits of practicing active listening as a manager?

4. List one tip for improving written communication skills.

5. What is one guideline for delivering impactful presentations?

6. Why is it important to use professional email etiquette?

7. What role does nonverbal communication play in verbal communication?

5Marks:

1 Explain how clear and effective communication impacts organizational culture and productivity?

2 Describe the key aspects of active listening and its importance in managerial roles.

3 Discuss the importance of providing constructive feedback and maintaining transparency in communication.

4 How can managers use persuasive communication techniques to influence stakeholders and drive organizational change?

5 Explain the significance of using visual aids and media in presentations. How can they enhance audience engagement and comprehension?

6 How can managers effectively handle Q&A sessions and feedback during presentations to reinforce key messages and address audience concerns?

Case Study: Enhancing Communication and Presentation Skills at ABC Enterprises

Background: ABC Enterprises is a mid-sized manufacturing firm known for its high-quality products and strong market presence. The company has been growing steadily, with an increasing number of projects and a larger workforce. Despite this success, ABC Enterprises began experiencing significant internal communication challenges. These issues were affecting project timelines, team dynamics, and overall productivity. Management recognized the need for a strategic intervention to improve communication and presentation skills across the organization.

Problem Faced: The communication issues at ABC Enterprises manifested in several ways:

1. **Missed Deadlines:** Poor communication between departments and within teams led to misunderstandings about project timelines and responsibilities. As a result, deadlines were frequently missed, causing delays in production and delivery.
2. **Low Team Morale:** The lack of clear and effective communication created frustration among employees. Team members felt unheard and undervalued, leading to a decline in morale and engagement.
3. **Frequent Conflicts:** Miscommunication often escalated into conflicts, both within teams and between departments. These conflicts not only disrupted workflow but also created a tense and unproductive work environment.
4. **Ineffective Presentations:** Managers and team leaders struggled to convey ideas clearly during meetings and presentations. This hindered decision-making processes and stakeholder engagement, affecting the company's strategic initiatives.

Strategic Solution to Improve the Issues:

To address these communication challenges, ABC Enterprises implemented a comprehensive strategy focusing on improving both written and verbal communication skills, as well as enhancing presentation capabilities.

1. **Communication Training Programs:**
    - **Active Listening Workshops:** The company introduced active listening workshops to teach employees how to listen attentively, ask clarifying questions, and provide feedback. These workshops aimed to foster a culture of open dialogue and mutual respect.
    - **Clarity and Precision in Communication:** Training sessions were conducted to emphasize the importance of clear and precise language. Employees were taught to avoid jargon, use simple language, and ensure their messages were easily understood.

2. **Improving Written Communication:**
    - **Professional Email Etiquette:** Workshops on professional email etiquette were held to guide employees on crafting clear, concise, and respectful emails. Topics included appropriate subject lines, structuring emails logically, and timely responses.
    - **Document Formatting and Grammar:** Sessions on document formatting and grammar were organized to enhance the professionalism of written communication. Employees learned to use consistent formatting, headings, bullet points, and proper grammar and punctuation.
3. **Enhancing Verbal Communication:**
    - **Public Speaking and Presentation Skills:** The company offered public speaking and presentation skills workshops. These sessions focused on voice modulation, body language, and engaging storytelling techniques to help managers and team leaders present their ideas effectively.
    - **Conflict Resolution Training:** Managers were trained in conflict resolution techniques, equipping them with the skills to navigate and resolve conflicts through constructive dialogue and open communication.
4. **Utilizing Technology:**
    - **Task Management Tools:** ABC Enterprises adopted task management tools like Trello and Asana to improve coordination and communication within teams. These tools helped in tracking progress, setting deadlines, and ensuring accountability.
    - **Digital Collaboration Platforms:** The company implemented digital collaboration platforms such as Microsoft Teams and Slack to facilitate real-time communication, file sharing, and virtual meetings.

Results and Impact:

The strategic initiatives led to significant improvements in communication and presentation skills at ABC Enterprises:

- **Increased Productivity:** Clear and effective communication helped streamline workflows, resulting in timely completion of projects and increased productivity.
- **Enhanced Team Morale:** Improved communication practices fostered a positive work environment, boosting team morale and employee engagement.
- **Reduced Conflicts:** Conflict resolution training and active listening skills led to fewer misunderstandings and conflicts, promoting a collaborative work culture.
- **Effective Presentations:** Managers and team leaders became more confident and persuasive in their presentations, leading to better decision-making and stakeholder engagement.

Overall, the comprehensive approach to enhancing communication and presentation skills empowered ABC Enterprises to achieve its strategic goals, improve employee satisfaction, and maintain a competitive edge in the market.

Ethics and Professionalism

Ethics and professionalism are foundational aspects of managerial roles, guiding decision-making, behaviour, and organizational culture. This module explores ethical considerations in managerial decision-making and behaviour, emphasizes the importance of maintaining integrity and professionalism, and uses case studies or scenarios to facilitate ethical reasoning and decision-making.

1. Ethical Considerations in Managerial Decision-Making and Behaviour:

Ethical considerations play a pivotal role in managerial decision-making, influencing organizational values, stakeholder trust, and long-term sustainability. Managers are entrusted with making decisions that impact stakeholders, including employees, customers, shareholders, and the broader community. Upholding ethical principles ensures fairness, transparency, and accountability in managerial roles.

Key Ethical Considerations:

1. **Ethical Frameworks**: Apply ethical frameworks, such as utilitarianism, deontology, virtue ethics, or ethical relativism, to evaluate moral dilemmas and guide decision-making. Ethical frameworks provide principles and guidelines for assessing the consequences, duties, virtues, or cultural context of ethical decisions.
2. **Stakeholder Impact**: Consider the interests, rights, and well-being of stakeholders affected by managerial decisions. Balance competing interests, prioritize stakeholders' concerns, and promote ethical behaviour that contributes to positive outcomes for all parties involved.
3. **Transparency and Accountability**: Foster a culture of transparency, honesty, and accountability in organizational practices and decision-making processes. Communicate openly with stakeholders, disclose relevant information, and take responsibility for the consequences of managerial decisions.

4. **Conflict of Interest**: Identify and manage conflicts of interest that may influence decision-making or compromise integrity. Implement policies, disclosure requirements, and ethical guidelines to mitigate conflicts of interest and uphold ethical standards.
5. **Legal Compliance**: Ensure compliance with legal requirements, regulations, and industry standards in managerial practices and decision-making. Adhere to ethical codes of conduct, professional standards, and corporate governance principles to prevent unethical behaviour and legal liabilities.
6. **Ethical Leadership**: Demonstrate ethical leadership by setting a positive example, promoting ethical behaviour, and fostering a culture of integrity within the organization. Encourage ethical decision-making among employees, recognize ethical dilemmas, and provide guidance on ethical principles and values.

2. Importance of Maintaining Integrity and Professionalism:

Maintaining integrity and professionalism is fundamental to earning trust, credibility, and respect as a manager. Integrity encompasses honesty, consistency, and adherence to ethical principles, while professionalism entails demonstrating competence, reliability, and ethical conduct in professional roles and interactions.

Key Aspects of Integrity and Professionalism:

1. **Trustworthiness**: Build trust with stakeholders through consistent honesty, transparency, and reliability in actions and decisions. Uphold commitments, fulfil responsibilities, and maintain ethical standards to foster trust and confidence in managerial leadership.
2. **Ethical Role Modelling**: Serve as a role model for ethical behaviour and professionalism within the organization. Demonstrate integrity in challenging situations, uphold ethical values, and inspire others to act ethically in their professional roles.
3. **Accountability**: Take ownership of actions, decisions, and outcomes, accepting responsibility for mistakes and learning from setbacks. Accountability reinforces integrity, promotes

transparency, and enhances organizational credibility and reputation.

4. **Respect and Fairness**: Treat others with respect, fairness, and dignity in professional interactions and decision-making processes. Value diverse perspectives, uphold human rights, and promote inclusivity to create a positive and respectful work environment.

5. **Confidentiality**: Safeguard confidential information, proprietary data, and sensitive disclosures to protect stakeholders' privacy and uphold professional standards. Adhere to confidentiality agreements, data protection policies, and ethical guidelines to maintain trust and confidentiality.

6. **Professional Development**: Invest in continuous learning, professional development, and ethical training to enhance competence, skills, and ethical decision-making capabilities. Stay informed about industry trends, ethical challenges, and best practices to uphold professionalism and adapt to evolving ethical standards.

3. Case Studies or Scenarios to Facilitate Ethical Reasoning and Decision-Making

Case studies or scenarios provide practical examples and ethical dilemmas that challenge managers to apply ethical reasoning, evaluate alternatives, and make informed decisions. Analyzing case studies enhances ethical awareness, decision-making skills, and the ability to navigate complex ethical challenges in managerial roles.

Benefits of Case Studies for Ethical Reasoning:

1. **Real-World Context**: Present real-world situations, dilemmas, and ethical challenges encountered in managerial practice. Case studies provide context, complexity, and relevance to ethical decision-making scenarios, allowing managers to analyze implications and consider diverse perspectives.

2. **Critical Thinking**: Promote critical thinking skills by analyzing case details, identifying ethical issues, and evaluating potential consequences of different courses of action. Encourage managers to weigh ethical considerations, apply ethical

frameworks, and justify their decisions based on ethical principles.

3. **Discussion and Debate**: Facilitate group discussions, debates, or role-playing exercises to explore different viewpoints, ethical perspectives, and decision-making strategies. Engage participants in collaborative dialogue, ethical debates, and ethical dilemma resolution to enhance learning and decision-making skills.

4. **Ethical Judgment**: Develop ethical judgment and decision-making competence by challenging managers to prioritize ethical values, principles, and stakeholder interests. Encourage reflection on personal values, ethical responsibilities, and the ethical implications of managerial decisions.

5. **Learning from Mistakes**: Analyze ethical dilemmas, ethical lapses, or ethical misconduct in case studies to learn from mistakes, identify root causes, and implement preventive measures. Use case studies as learning opportunities to improve ethical awareness, decision-making processes, and organizational ethics.

By integrating ethical considerations into managerial decision-making, emphasizing the importance of integrity and professionalism, and using case studies to facilitate ethical reasoning, managers can uphold ethical standards, foster a culture of integrity, and make ethical decisions that contribute to organizational success and stakeholder trust. These practices promote ethical leadership, enhance organizational reputation, and ensure sustainable business practices aligned with ethical principles and values.

Question Bank:

2 Marks:

1. What are the key ethical considerations that influence managerial decision-making?

2. How can managers demonstrate ethical leadership within an organization?

3. Why is maintaining transparency and accountability important in managerial roles?

4. What role does conflict of interest play in ethical decision-making, and how can it be managed?

5. How can ethical frameworks such as utilitarianism and deontology guide managerial decisions?

5Marks:

1. Why is confidentiality crucial in maintaining professionalism and trust within an organization?

2. How can case studies facilitate ethical reasoning and decision-making for managers?

3. Discuss the importance of integrating ethical considerations into managerial decision-making and its impact on organizational values, stakeholder trust, and long-term sustainability. Provide examples to support your answer.

4. Explain the concept of ethical leadership and its significance in promoting a culture of integrity within an organization. How can managers serve as ethical role models for their teams?

5. Analyze the importance of maintaining integrity and professionalism in earning trust, credibility, and respect as a manager. Include examples of how integrity and professionalism can influence managerial effectiveness.

10 Marks:

1. Explore the challenges and solutions in managing conflicts of interest within an organization. How can policies, disclosure requirements, and ethical guidelines mitigate conflicts of interest?

2. Discuss the role of transparency and accountability in fostering a positive organizational culture. How can managers communicate openly with stakeholders and take responsibility for their decisions?

3. Evaluate the benefits of using case studies or scenarios in training programs to enhance ethical reasoning and decision-making skills for managers. Provide examples of how case studies can develop critical thinking and ethical judgment.

4. Explain how continuous learning, professional development, and ethical training can enhance managerial competence and ethical decision-making capabilities. How can managers stay informed about industry trends, ethical challenges, and best practices?

Module 11

Continuous Learning and Development

Continuous learning and development are essential for managers to adapt to evolving industry trends, expand professional capabilities, and achieve long-term career growth. This module explores the mindset of lifelong learning and professional growth, strategies for staying updated on industry trends and best practices, and resources for ongoing development, including courses, books, and networking opportunities.

1. The Mindset of Lifelong Learning and Professional Growth

The mindset of lifelong learning is characterized by a commitment to acquiring new knowledge, developing skills, and fostering personal and professional growth throughout one's career. Embracing continuous learning enables managers to stay relevant in a rapidly changing business environment, innovate in their roles, and enhance organizational effectiveness.

Key Aspects of the Mindset of Lifelong Learning:

1. **Curiosity and Adaptability**: Cultivate curiosity to explore new ideas, perspectives, and emerging trends in the industry. Embrace change, adapt to technological advancements, and seek opportunities for innovation and continuous improvement.
2. **Self-Motivation and Initiative**: Take initiative to pursue learning opportunities, set professional development goals, and invest in skill enhancement. Demonstrate self-motivation, resilience, and a proactive approach to continuous learning and career advancement.
3. **Reflection and Self-Assessment**: Reflect on personal strengths, areas for improvement, and learning objectives to identify skill gaps and development needs. Conduct self-assessments, seek feedback from peers and mentors, and prioritize areas for professional growth.

4. **Commitment to Excellence**: Strive for excellence in professional roles and responsibilities by acquiring relevant knowledge, mastering skills, and applying best practices. Maintain high standards of performance, continuous improvement, and ethical conduct in pursuit of career goals.

5. **Adaptive Learning Strategies**: Adapt learning strategies to individual preferences, learning styles, and career aspirations. Explore diverse learning methods, such as workshops, seminars, online courses, or experiential learning opportunities, to enhance knowledge acquisition and skill development.

6. **Resilience and Persistence**: Embrace challenges, setbacks, and learning opportunities as essential components of professional growth. Build resilience, persevere through obstacles, and view failures as learning experiences that contribute to personal and professional development.

2. Strategies for Staying Updated on Industry Trends and Best Practices

Staying updated on industry trends and best practices is crucial for managers to anticipate market changes, leverage emerging opportunities, and maintain competitive advantage. Implementing effective strategies for continuous learning and staying informed empowers managers to make informed decisions, drive innovation, and lead organizational change.

Effective Strategies for Staying Updated:

1. **Industry Research and Monitoring**: Conduct regular industry research, monitor market trends, and analyze competitive landscapes to stay informed about emerging technologies, consumer preferences, and industry developments. Use market reports, industry publications, and reputable sources for up-to-date information.

2. **Professional Networking**: Build and maintain professional networks with industry peers, thought leaders, and subject matter experts to exchange knowledge, share insights, and stay informed about industry trends. Attend industry conferences,

networking events, and forums to foster connections and expand professional contacts.

3. **Continuous Education and Training**: Enroll in professional development courses, certifications, or workshops to acquire new skills, update industry knowledge, and enhance professional competencies. Invest in lifelong learning opportunities offered by educational institutions, professional associations, or online learning platforms.

4. **Thought Leadership and Thought Partnerships**: Follow thought leaders, industry influencers, and reputable sources of thought leadership content to gain insights, perspectives, and best practices. Engage in thought partnerships, collaborative projects, or advisory roles to contribute expertise, share knowledge, and exchange innovative ideas.

5. **Cross-Functional Collaboration**: Collaborate with cross-functional teams, departments, or business units to leverage diverse perspectives, share expertise, and foster interdisciplinary learning. Participate in cross-functional projects, task forces, or innovation initiatives to broaden industry knowledge and cultivate collaborative relationships.

6. **Technology Adoption and Innovation**: Embrace technology adoption, digital transformation, and innovative practices within the industry. Stay updated on technological advancements, disruptive innovations, and industry-specific applications to enhance operational efficiency and drive organizational growth

3. Resources for Ongoing Development: Courses, Books, and Networking

Accessing diverse resources for ongoing development, including courses, books, and networking opportunities, enriches managers' professional growth, expands knowledge base, and enhances career prospects in dynamic industries.

Key Resources for Ongoing Development:

1. **Professional Development Courses**: Enrol in professional development courses, workshops, or seminars offered by educational institutions, industry associations, or corporate

training programs. Choose courses aligned with career goals, skill enhancement objectives, and emerging industry trends.

2. **Skill-Based Training Programs**: Participate in skill-based training programs, certifications, or bootcamps to develop specialized skills, acquire technical expertise, and stay updated on industry-specific practices. Enhance proficiency in areas such as leadership, project management, digital marketing, or data analytics.

3. **Online Learning Platforms**: Access online learning platforms, such as Coursera, LinkedIn Learning, or Udemy, to explore a wide range of courses, tutorials, and micro-learning modules. Leverage flexible learning formats, self-paced study options, and interactive content to accommodate professional schedules and learning preferences.

4. **Industry-Specific Books and Publications**: Read industry-specific books, journals, articles, and publications to deepen knowledge, gain insights into industry trends, and stay informed about best practices. Explore reputable sources, thought-provoking literature, and influential authors to expand professional expertise and stimulate critical thinking.

5. **Networking Events and Conferences**: Attend networking events, industry conferences, and professional gatherings to connect with peers, expand professional contacts, and engage in knowledge-sharing activities. Participate in panel discussions, keynote presentations, or workshops to exchange ideas, learn from industry experts, and explore emerging trends.

6. **Mentorship and Coaching Programs**: Seek mentorship or coaching from experienced professionals, industry leaders, or mentors within the organization. Benefit from personalized guidance, career advice, and professional development insights to navigate career challenges, overcome obstacles, and achieve career aspirations.

By cultivating a mindset of lifelong learning, implementing strategies for staying updated on industry trends, and leveraging resources for ongoing development, managers can enhance professional growth, adapt to changing business environments, and contribute to organizational success through continuous innovation and knowledge advancement. Embrace opportunities for learning, explore diverse learning resources, and commit to lifelong development to excel in managerial roles and make meaningful contributions to organizational excellence.

Case Study: Continuous Learning and Development

Background:

TechSavvy Solutions is a mid-sized software development company specializing in custom enterprise software solutions. The company has been successful over the past decade, thanks to its ability to deliver high-quality products tailored to client needs. However, with rapid advancements in technology and increasing competition, the company's leadership recognized the need for continuous learning and development to maintain its competitive edge. The company's management team, led by CEO Jane Collins, decided to implement a comprehensive learning and development strategy.

Problems Faced:

1. **Technological Advancements**: The fast pace of technological change meant that many employees were working with outdated knowledge and skills, impacting productivity and innovation.
2. **Employee Retention**: Talented employees were leaving the company for opportunities offering better professional development, leading to high turnover rates.
3. **Industry Trends and Best Practices**: The company struggled to keep up with emerging industry trends and best practices, which affected its ability to innovate and stay competitive.
4. **Knowledge Silos**: There was limited cross-functional collaboration, leading to knowledge silos and inefficiencies within the organization

Strategic Solutions:

1. **Cultivating a Lifelong Learning Mindset:**
   - **Curiosity and Adaptability**: The company encouraged a culture of curiosity by organizing monthly innovation days where employees could explore new technologies

and present their findings. This initiative fostered adaptability and innovation.

- o **Self-Motivation and Initiative**: Employees were incentivized to pursue professional development goals through recognition programs and career advancement opportunities.

2. **Staying Updated on Industry Trends and Best Practices**:
   - o **Industry Research and Monitoring**: TechSavvy Solutions subscribed to leading industry publications and utilized market research tools to stay informed about technological advancements and market trends. The company also established a dedicated team to analyze competitive landscapes and identify opportunities for innovation.
   - o **Professional Networking**: Employees were encouraged to attend industry conferences, webinars, and networking events. The company provided stipends for travel and registration fees to ensure broad participation.

3. **Providing Resources for Ongoing Development**:
   - o **Professional Development Courses**: The company partnered with local universities and online learning platforms like Coursera and LinkedIn Learning to offer employees access to a wide range of courses. Employees could select courses aligned with their career goal and emerging industry trends.
   - o **Skill-Based Training Programs**: TechSavvy Solutions introduced in-house training programs and certifications in critical areas such as cloud computing, artificial intelligence, and project management. These programs were designed to enhance technical expertise and keep employees updated on industry-specific practices.
   - o **Online Learning Platforms**: Employees were given access to online learning platforms, allowing them to engage in self-paced learning. This flexibility helped employees balance their professional and personal commitments while pursuing continuous development.
   - o **Mentorship and Coaching Programs**: The company implemented mentorship programs where experienced

professionals provided personalized guidance to less experienced employees. This initiative helped in career development and knowledge sharing across the organization.

4. **Enhancing Cross-Functional Collaboration**:
   - **Cross-Functional Projects**: The company initiated cross-functional projects and task forces to encourage collaboration between different departments. This approach helped break down knowledge silos and promoted interdisciplinary learning.
   - **Technology Adoption and Innovation**: TechSavvy Solutions embraced digital transformation by implementing collaborative tools and platforms that facilitated knowledge sharing and innovation. Regular workshops and hackathons were organized to drive technological advancements within the company

Outcomes:

By adopting a comprehensive continuous learning and development strategy, TechSavvy Solutions experienced several positive outcomes. Employee retention rates improved significantly, and the company attracted top talent due to its commitment to professional development. The organization became more agile and innovative, staying ahead of industry trends and maintaining a competitive edge. Enhanced cross-functional collaboration led to increased efficiency and the successful delivery of innovative solutions to clients. Ultimately, TechSavvy Solutions solidified its reputation as a forward-thinking and dynamic organization committed to continuous learning and development.

Question Bank:

2 Marks Questions:

1. What is the mindset of lifelong learning?

2. Why is adaptability important in continuous learning?

3. How can self-assessment help in professional growth?

4. What role does curiosity play in a manager's development?

5. Name two strategies for staying updated on industry trends.

5 Marks Questions:

1. Explain how cultivating a mindset of lifelong learning can enhance a manager's effectiveness in a rapidly changing business environment.

2. Discuss the key aspects of the mindset of lifelong learning and how they contribute to professional growth.

3. Describe the effective strategies for staying updated on industry trends and best practices. How do these strategies empower managers to lead organizational change?

4. How can cross-functional collaboration contribute to a manager's ongoing development and organizational success?

5. Analyze the role of professional networking in continuous learning and development. Provide examples of how networking can enhance career growth.

10 Marks Questions:

1. Discuss the importance of technology adoption and innovation in continuous learning. How can managers stay updated on technological advancements?

2. Evaluate the different resources available for ongoing development, such as courses, books, and networking opportunities. How can managers leverage these resources to achieve long-term career growth?

Module 12

Conclusion and Action Plan

The conclusion and action plan module serve as a culmination of the managerial skills handbook, summarizing key takeaways, providing actionable steps for applying managerial skills in daily practice, and offering self-assessment tools or reflection questions to gauge personal growth and development.

1. Summary of Key Takeaways from the Handbook

Throughout the handbook on managerial skills, several key takeaways emerge that are essential for effective leadership and management in contemporary organizational settings. These takeaways encapsulate the foundational principles, strategies, and practices discussed across various modules:

Foundational Managerial Skills:

- **Technical Skills**: Mastery of functional expertise in areas such as marketing, finance, operations, and technology is crucial for effective decision-making and operational efficiency.
- **Human Relations Skills**: Effective communication, empathy, conflict resolution, teamwork, and motivation are critical for fostering positive relationships and team cohesion.
- **Conceptual Skills**: Strategic thinking, long-term planning, and decision-making at different managerial levels enable leaders to align organizational goals with market dynamics and competitive landscapes.
- **Global Management Skills**: Cross-cultural competence, international business acumen, and managing diverse teams are vital for navigating global business environments and leveraging global opportunities.

Leadership and Influence:

- **Effective Leadership Characteristics**: Traits such as integrity, vision, adaptability, and resilience are foundational to inspiring and guiding teams toward achieving organizational goals.
- **Leadership Styles**: Different leadership styles, including transformational, transactional, and servant leadership, impact team performance and organizational culture differently.

Problem-Solving and Decision-Making:

- **Systematic Frameworks**: Utilizing frameworks for systematic problem-solving and decision-making enhances efficiency and effectiveness in addressing organizational challenges.
- **Information Gathering and Analysis**: Methods for gathering relevant information, analyzing options, and implementing solutions are critical for informed decision-making.

Time and Stress Management:

- **Prioritization and Time Management**: Strategies for prioritizing tasks, managing time effectively, and minimizing distractions are essential for optimizing productivity and achieving work-life balance.
- **Stress Reduction Techniques**: Techniques such as mindfulness, physical exercise, and healthy lifestyle choices mitigate stress and enhance well-being.

Ethics and Professionalism:

- **Ethical Decision-Making**: Considering ethical implications in managerial decision-making fosters trust, transparency, and organizational integrity.
- **Maintaining Integrity**: Upholding professionalism, accountability, and respect in all professional interactions and decisions is crucial for organizational credibility.

Continuous Learning and Development:

- **Lifelong Learning Mindset**: Embracing a mindset of continuous learning, self-motivation, and adaptive learning strategies fosters personal growth and professional development.
- **Staying Updated**: Strategies such as industry research, professional networking, and ongoing education enable managers to stay informed about industry trends and best practices.

2. Actionable Steps for Applying Managerial Skills in Daily Practice

To translate theoretical knowledge into practical application, managers can implement actionable steps based on the key takeaways from the handbook:

Implementation Strategies:

1. **Integrate Skills into Daily Routine**: Incorporate technical, human relations, conceptual, and global management skills into daily tasks and responsibilities.
2. **Set SMART Goals**: Establish Specific, Measurable, Achievable, Relevant, and Time-bound goals aligned with organizational objectives and personal development aspirations.
3. **Practice Leadership Principles**: Apply effective leadership characteristics and styles to inspire teams, foster innovation, and achieve performance goals.
4. **Utilize Problem-Solving Frameworks**: Implement systematic frameworks for problem-solving and decision-making to address challenges methodically.
5. **Manage Time and Stress Effectively**: Implement strategies for prioritizing tasks, managing time, reducing stress, and maintaining work-life balance to enhance productivity and well-being.
6. **Promote Ethical Behavior**: Integrate ethical considerations into decision-making processes, uphold integrity, and promote ethical behavior within the organization.
7. **Commit to Continuous Learning**: Pursue ongoing learning opportunities, stay updated on industry trends, and invest in professional development to expand skills and knowledge base.

3. Self-Assessment Tools or Reflection Questions to Gauge Personal Growth and Development

Self-assessment tools and reflection questions facilitate introspection, evaluation, and continuous improvement in managerial skills and professional development:

Self-Assessment Areas:

1. **Technical Skills**: Evaluate proficiency in specific technical areas relevant to managerial responsibilities. Reflect on strengths, areas for improvement, and opportunities for skill enhancement.
2. **Leadership Effectiveness**: Assess leadership capabilities, including communication, decision-making, team management, and conflict resolution skills.
3. **Problem-Solving Abilities**: Reflect on past decision-making processes, problem-solving approaches, and outcomes. Identify strengths in analytical thinking and areas for refining problem-solving strategies.
4. **Time and Stress Management**: Evaluate time management practices, stress levels, and effectiveness in achieving work-life balance. Identify stress triggers, implement stress reduction techniques, and optimize time allocation.
5. **Ethical Decision-Making**: Reflect on ethical dilemmas encountered, decisions made, and adherence to ethical principles. Assess consistency in ethical behavior, transparency, and accountability.
6. **Continuous Learning Progress**: Review participation in professional development activities, acquisition of new skills, and application of learning in professional roles. Set goals for continuous learning and career advancement.

Reflection Questions:

- How have I applied managerial skills learned from this handbook in my professional role?
- What are my strengths in leadership, problem-solving, and decision-making?

- How can I enhance my technical expertise in specific functional areas?
- What strategies have I implemented to manage time effectively and reduce stress?
- How do I uphold ethical standards and professionalism in my interactions and decision-making?
- What learning opportunities have I pursued to stay updated on industry trends and best practices?
- What are my career goals, and what steps can I take to achieve them through continuous learning and development?

By reflecting on these self-assessment tools and questions, managers can gauge personal growth, identify areas for improvement, and develop action plans to enhance managerial skills, drive organizational success, and achieve professional excellence. Continuous reflection, learning, and application of managerial skills enable managers to adapt to evolving challenges, lead with confidence, and contribute effectively to organizational goals and objectives.